Herschell Gordon Lewis

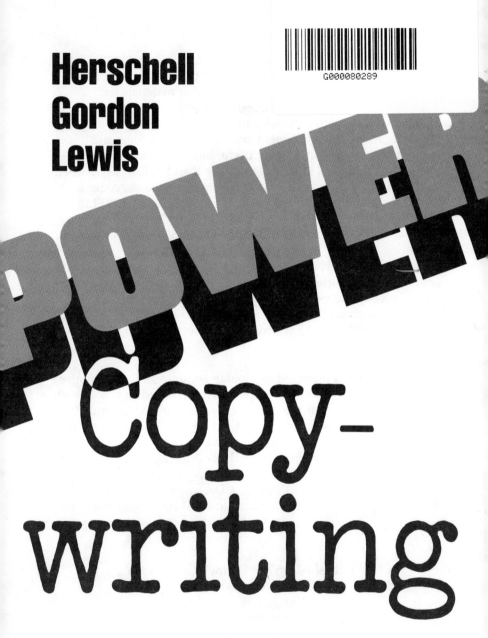

POWER

Copy-writing

DYNAMIC NEW COMMUNICATIONS TECHNIQUES TO HELP YOU SELL MORE PRODUCTS AND SERVICES

Dartnell is a publisher serving the world of business with books, manuals, newsletters, bulletins, and training materials for executives, managers, supervisors, salespeople, financial officials, human resources professionals, and office employees. In addition, Dartnell produces management and sales training films and audiocassettes, publishes many useful business forms, and offers many of its materials in languages other than English. Established in 1917, Dartnell serves the world's complete business community. For catalogs and product information write: THE DARTNELL CORPORATION, 4660 Ravenswood Avenue, Chicago, Illinois 60640-4595 USA. Phone 800-621-5463. In Illinois: (312) 561-4000.

This publication is designed to provide accurate and authoritative information in regard to the subject matter covered. It is sold with the understanding that the publisher is not engaged in rendering legal, accounting, or other professional service. If legal advice or other expert assistance is required, the services of a competent professional person should be sought.

From a Declaration of Principles jointly adopted by a Committee of the American Bar Association and a Committee of Publishers.

Published by The Dartnell Corporation
4660 Ravenswood Avenue
Chicago, Illinois 60640
Chicago/Boston/London/Sydney

© 1992 Dartnell Corporation
ISBN 0-85013-187-1
Library of Congress Catalog Card Number: 91-076596
Printed in the USA by The Dartnell Press
10 9 8 7 6 5 4 3 2 1

Table of Contents

With Color at Hand, Why Write in Black and White? **2** . . . The
1970s and 1980s Are History, Not Current Thinking. But Human
Motivations Don't Change (Thank Goodness) **3** . . . Separating
Wheat from Chaff **6** . . . Optimizing Information **7** . . . The
Clarity Commandment **10** . . . Clarity, Argot, and Verisimili-
tude **11** . . . Remember Who Your Reader Is **12** . . . We Know
How to Write. Do We Know How to Sell? **15** . . . Rats in a
Maze **15** . . . Invasion of the Phrase-Snatchers **18** . . . The
Doublespeak Diversion **19** . . . Synonyms Aren't Synonymous **20**
. . . Keep Your Weapon Sharp, Whoever You Are! **21**

The Rule of Numerical Manipulation **23** . . . Decimals or
Fractions **24** . . . When to Avoid Using *No.* for *Number* **25** . . . Plus
vs. Minus **25** . . . The Generic Determination Rule **26** . . . Strings
of Numbers vs. Fractions **27** . . . Zeros Add the Impression
of Size **28** . . . $200 a Day? $6,000 a Month? $70,000 a Year? **28**
. . . The Subrule of Numerical Manipulation **29** . . . Statistics
Don't Sell **32** . . . Give Numbers "Breathing Room" **35** . . . When
and How Much to Underline **38** . . . The Power in Quotation
Marks **41** . . . Parentheses to Suggest Exclusivity **45** . . . Parentheses as Asterisk Replacements and De-Emphasizers **46** . . . Paren-
theses to Replace *Such As* **47** . . . Parentheses to Keep Your Target
Smiling **48** . . . Replacing Commas with "And" **49** . . . Replacing
Periods with "And" **49** . . . The Pros and Cons of Abbreviations **49**
. . . Less Is More in Exclamation Points **50** . . . Dash, Ellipsis,

Foreword

Since beginning this book, I've become more aware of a curiosity you also may have experienced: The difference between extemporaneous speaking and thoughtful writing isn't specificity; it's the method of power-injection.

An accomplished speaker can add power to a communication without a heavy-duty knowledge of word use. Knowledge of word use is a writer-weapon. Parallel speaker-weapons are voice inflection, practiced pauses, sped-up or slowed-down delivery, and alternation of shouting, whispering, and straightforward talk.

The writer has none of these auxiliaries. It's murder trying to be a demagogue in print. We have to master the science of word *use*, not the far easier, far more primitive art of word *delivery*.

So a speaker can begin with "There are . . ." or "It is my privilege to . . ." and not run afoul of principles of power communication. The writer who uses these same openings is ignoring the dissimilarity of weaponry.

Each of us has (Every one of us has? All of us have? We've all? The meanings are close but not identical) read a piece of copy to a client, a boss, a business associate. Do we read it "flat," uninflected, the way a computer voice might read it? Do we limit emphasis to underlined words? Probably not. We read it the way we talk.

So we cheat, even as we ask for an opinion of the words we've written.

A better way: Ambience-for-ambience. No cheating by artificial verbalized pumping up, if you're a genuine power communicator. And you are, or you wouldn't be bothering to read *this* blather.

Two 21st Century Words: Information Optimizing

A suggestion—memorize two words and you'll be a worthy competitor in the year 2010:

Information optimizing.

This book begins a "codification" process. Please accept as just my own opinion: Over the next generation, being able to codify rules, to optimize information, will give writers the edge they deserve, over their target-readers, viewers, or listeners.

How? Because "force-communication"—*power* communication—enables us to effect minuscule attitude-changes without altering the factual base. A word change here, a phrase change there, and the power of your selling message increases by a couple of volts.

As the red-hot concept of information optimizing gets even hotter, anticipate hordes of "would-be" practitioners hurling themselves against the barbed wire of knowledge separating us from the elementary seat-of-the-pants communications world we shared with them before we knew better.

To keep them out of Eden—and ourselves in—all we have to do is write or speak more effectively than they do.

Easy! We drop a *that* here . . . we change *would* to *will* there . . . we never use *purchase* as a verb . . . we transform the arm's-length *requested* to the mild grammatical outrage *asked for* . . . we struggle into our Conviviality Masks . . . and we're in overdrive while they're still struggling to get out of low gear. So . . .

"Good-bye to 'Seat of the Pants' Communications? Awwww . . . "

If you're a hard-bitten data-driven marketing writer who feels raw description will sell your product or service, I'm about to rain on your party.

Your position had validity 200 years ago, when both marketing and its step-nephew advertising were neither organized nor duplicitous. If you were selling your horse, your notice posted on a tree or in the town square would say, "Horse for Sale." If the horse were spavined, the notice would say, "Spavined Horse for Sale," or you'd be too busy picking off tar and feathers to be able to post another sign.

Today's marketplace is shot through with skepticism. Our job isn't just to announce what we have for sale. We say, "Horse for—" and our target cuts us off: "Not interested."

Even a tyro can regurgitate facts; a reasonably proficient writer can describe. Olympus belongs to those who don't settle for re-telling of facts or photographic physical descriptions . . . those whose word choices generate tiny bubbles of desire, bubbles the reader may not even know are effervescing.

Why is the ability to refine word choices such a key to the future of force-communication? In my opinion it's because constant exposure to media messages has eroded any vestiges of trust and faith and replaced those kind and gentle elements with harsh skepticism.

Today's Ambience: The Age of Skepticism

We're wallowing in the Age of Skepticism. Readers, viewers, and listeners are trained to *dis*believe any message they think represents a self-serving attitude . . . and they (they? no, we—all of us!) assume *every* message represents a self-serving attitude.

Frustrated advertisers aggravate their own wounds, widening the gap between seller and sellee by depending on *bulk*, not power. The assumption—backed by realistic fear of clutter in conventional media—is an anachronism, a throwback to the old "volume = impact" notion of Watsonian Behaviorism, a concept of the 1930s. Hey, my friends, it just doesn't work.

If the people who spend the most money sell the most, it's because they connected, not because they spent the most money. Advertising agencies create noncommunicating campaigns that may bring applause inside the office; how about *outside* the office? (Direct marketers have an edge over advertisers whose relationship with the buyer *isn't* direct: their unassailable method of scorekeeping: We connected . . . or we didn't connect.)

So the ability to add a slight warp to a communication will be—in my opinion—the great separator of the early 21st century. Readers will divide communicators who bombard them with messages of varying relevance into three categories: apprentice . . . journeyman . . . meistersinger. That highest level will be the exclusive domain of the power copywriter.

Even if I'm wrong, I'm *not* wrong in assuming we communicators should tighten every rhetorical bolt if we want to justify the adjective *professional* as a modifier of the noun *writer.*

It's not only simplistic to say we have to describe what the buyer wants to buy, not what we want to sell. It's also a wrong interpretation of power copywriting.

Are you 100 percent determined to maximize your chance (not your "opportunity," typifying exactly what this whole notion is about) to cause the right target to jerk on the wire when you increase the voltage? Then you'll look for ways to optimize your message *sentence by sentence*. But the writer who keeps polishing right through the silver-plating doesn't warrant a round of applause.

When you're grinding out dozens of messages each year, polishing isn't as practical—or useful, for that matter—as knowing why you're looking for hidden cracks in your sales argument, the way an X-ray machine looks for hidden flaws in the metal skins of airplanes.

If you feel, as I do, that the future of communication dominance lies in the keyboard-poised hands of those who really care about the difference between "chance" and "opportunity." . . .

Let your next communication lie fallow for a day, after writing it. Then edit it, making word changes you think add a smidgeon of impact here, a touch of clarity there. *As you make the changes*, ask yourself, "Why am I doing this? Why is the change superior to the words I originally wrote?"

At least once or twice during this revealment procedure, you'll codify what you used to accept subliminally into your own Power Copywriting Point.

I predict (with the happy-go-lucky confidence that always attends blind speculation): We're close to the period word-historians will describe as The Era of Power Communication.

Now, I could have written, "We aren't far from the period word-historians will describe as The Era of Power Communication."

This choice of phraseology—"close" instead of "not far"—is one small step for the power copywriter. Right step or wrong step?

Much of the whole notion of power copywriting defies that question. It's out of phase, because in most cases the choice isn't "right" or "wrong"; it's ☐ "acceptable" or ☐ "slightly better" or

☐ "considerably better" or ☐ "substantially better" than accept-able. We're professionals, and we aren't about to develop a case of foot-in-mouth disease. The difference isn't between commu-nicating and *non*-communicating; it's between communicating and *power*-communicating. Had I written, "We're close—very close—to the period word-historians will describe as the Era of Power Communication," I wouldn't have tinkered with the thrust of the message; I'd have been trying to fine-tune the power.

If by 2001 we don't have a dozen computer programs geared to this type of refinement, I'll be more than surprised. I'll be disappointed. We now have a dozen or more programs attacking grammar and style; why not software directed at power?

Every writer who survives his or her first few years in the roiling seas of advertising, public relations, or any other marketing-related creative function knows some rhetorical tricks.

Whether to write "a decade" or "ten years" . . . whether to write "Houston, San Antonio, Austin, and Dallas" or "Houston and San Antonio and Austin and Dallas" . . . whether to write "I'm writing you about" or "I write you about" . . . the decision flows out of the fingertips automatically.

Is it the right decision?

The word-artisan makes an educated guess. The word-jour-neyman makes an uneducated guess. The word-apprentice may choose the most persuasive direction—by accident.

The word-meistersinger doesn't guess. He or she uses prin-ciples . . . the principles for which this book makes just the first convulsive beginning. (Yes, you'll have answers to "Houston and San Antonio . . ." and "I'm writing you / I write you. . . .")

What's It All About, Alfie?

As you pick and choose among these power copywriting techniques, your reactions probably will rotate along four different but equally logical planes:

1. I knew that.
2. I didn't know that, but so what?
3. I didn't know that, and now I'm glad I do.
4. That point is so subtle it can't have much direct impact.

All four are valid, depending on how deeply your feet are stuck in the pleasant quagmire of *force*-communication. I bring up this set of reactions because I have to defend—no, extol—my own rationale for presenting information-cum-prejudices. Another wild opinion: They might result in a fractional percentage of improvement in response to something you write or say.

So, please, ignore the suggestions that generate a "no. 1" or "no. 2" reaction for you; welcome those that give you a "no. 3" reaction; and accept the "no. 4" propositions as curios for your word-cabinet, more entertaining than useful except when you're exhibiting your collection to a visitor.

Power copywriting—information optimizing—is as fascinating and as professional a concept as writers ever have been offered to enable them to maintain virtuoso-level performance. In my opinion, a working knowledge of power copywriting is as potent a weapon to persuasive writing as the laser is to medicine. It's the future. And all we have to do is the Verbal Two-Step:

1. We begin to realize that how we couch our phrases guides the reader's acceptance of those phrases.
2. We stare at what we've written or what somebody else has written or what we didn't write . . . and analyze, analyze, until we can clarify *why* one twist of words is more likely to motivate our readers than another.

(An example: What if, in the previous paragraph, the word *somebody* had been *someone*? Would the thought have been more dynamic or less dynamic? For that matter, what if the sentence you just read were split: "Would the thought have been more dynamic? Or less dynamic?" Impact does shift.)

Oh, sure, we can become so analytical our fingers are paralyzed. So we dare not get so hooked on power copywriting that it destroys the good old seat-of-the-pants ability that nudged us into this profession in the first place.

All right. We find a balance. I'll settle for recognition of power copywriting as a *concept*. Then we parallel beginning card players learning the game of bridge: Every day we master another rule or two, and before long we're writing the bridge column for the local paper.

A Note About Chapter Organization

Deciding where to put a particular reference is sometimes a matter of arbitrary choice. Some of the examples in Chapter 3, "Little Words Mean a Lot," might have been in Chapter 7, "Power Communication Through Throwaway Phrases."

The index will help when you're trying to relocate a specific reference. Otherwise you'll just have to take a look at both chapters . . . perhaps to find that the reference you want is in chapter 12.

Acknowledgments

I'm grateful to the publisher and editors of *Direct Marketing*, who let me try out some of the concepts in this book on the magazine's readers. Other bits and pieces appeared in *Catalog Age* and the British publication *Direct Marketing International*.

Rich Hagle, my most literate and patient editor at Dartnell, nursed this project, guiding it unerringly with only the subtlest of pressures no civilized author could resist. And Ellen Cleary, who converted the manuscript into a coherent format catching the inevitable typos and lapses, has my admiration and respect.

Carol Nelson, whom I regard as one of the natural leaders of the next generation of great copywriters, graciously read through the manuscript, making invaluable suggestions.

As usual, principal credit for this book appearing in print goes to my business partner, and inspirational goad, my wife and partner Margo, whose encouragement is beyond value.

Thank you all. And thank you, the reader, for trusting the concept enough to acquire this book.

Herschell Gordon Lewis
Plantation, Florida USA

Chapter 1
"What's This All About, Anyway?"

Sometimes I long for that golden bygone time when describing what we were offering could sell it. I even have a touch of nostalgia for the 1950s and 1960s when we could yell, "We're the best!"—and our yet-unsophisticated targets actually believed us.

No more. Our target-buyers have severed the umbilical cord that once tied them and us together regardless of our communicative ineptitude.

Cutting the umbilical cord underscores one of the regrettable truisms of any profession, including communication: Old-timers resist change.

That's why some of them brag about using the same old Underwood typewriter they used in school. That's why they claim flatly, without testing letter length, "If you can't say it in one page, you can't say it at all."

That's why they haven't updated their approach to combat the skepticism of the 1990s.

Absorption comes slowly but inexorably. If I didn't still get letters headed "Dear Sir or Madam," or "Gentlemen," I'd be able to make the happy claim that these antiquities have gone the way of the passenger pigeon and the dodo bird. No, they're more like the condor: They're dying out, but a handful of preservationists are keeping them alive.

Has communication changed all that much over the past ten years? If we're talking about *force-communication*, you bet it has! In fact, make it five years. For that matter, the day before yesterday isn't that recent.

With Color at Hand, Why Write in Black and White?

Once an unenlightened communicator realizes the whole concept of *power* means salesmanship, that communicator begins to use words enhancing what he or she has been selling, nuts-and-bolts generics.

Example: an ad for the Jan Hagara Collectors' Club. Bullet copy tells us what we get as members of this club. These are the bullets:

- A cloisonne membership pin.
- ID card.
- A year's subscription to the quarterly newsletter. (Worth more than the $22.50 alone!)
- A custom-designed 3-ring binder.
- Exclusive right to buy product available only to club members.

Each bullet has a rubber nose. Suppose *you* were writing this copy. Even if you'd never heard of this club, you probably would attack the benefits of membership with some enthusiasm.

Example:

- Genuine cloisonné membership pin.
- Personal, signed membership card.
- One full year's subscription to the quarterly News-letter. (This alone is worth more than one year's dues!)
- Custom binder to protect valuable Certificates and Newsletter.
- Exclusive offers available only to Club members.

Rationale: "A cloisonne membership pin" suggests minor worth. No exclusivity = no value. "Genuine" adds value, and even slapping the acute accent over the final *e* helps glorify this premium.

"ID card" is what you flash at the guard on your way to your job at the blast furnace in the steel mill. Where is implied value?

"A year's subscription" isn't as valuable as "one full year's subscription." The word "alone" is misplaced in the original; it should lead, not follow, so it modifies the right word. Capitalizing the word "Newsletter" adds importance. (We didn't attack another element, the "why": What makes this newsletter valuable? A specific would help here.)

"Custom-designed" and "3-ring binder" fight each other. We can buy 3-ring binders at the drug store. So we knock out "3-ring" and give the prospective member a reason for the binder. (Is "binder" our spiffiest word?)

"Product" is what we'd call a grab-bag of schlock items. We're writing about *art*.

This little example is a microcosm of what we're supposed to do for a living.

Example: We know an early reference sets the mood. An event will occur in three weeks. Three what-kind-of weeks? Three short weeks? Three endless weeks? Three sunny weeks? Three murderous weeks? Three happy weeks? If we're to be the architects of reader/viewer/listener reaction, we have to specify the building-blocks.

The 1970s and 1980s Are History, Not Current Thinking . . . But Human Motivations Don't Change (Thank Goodness)

In the "every day is different" world of communications creativity, rules are fluid. Yesterday's innovation is today's cliché.

If you don't believe this, re-read any book on marketing or copywriting (or for that matter, any form of communication) written during the 1970s. Most of the principles in them have to be adapted and updated. Their value is historical, not practical; judged by today's and tomorrow's effective marketing principles, they might as well have been written in the 1870s.

That isn't so terrible, though, because some concepts seem eternally youthful—especially those dealing in human motivation, which (because emotion outpunches intellect) changes slowly.

But techniques do change. Telemarketing was excitingly new just a few years ago; card decks were an innovation. Cable television home shopping shows were a novelty that might or might not grow beyond embryo.

Everyone who makes a living in any communications capacity has to update his or her thinking constantly—or be doomed to that unholy Weak Response Limbo where yesterday's ideas smolder without burning, like a not-quite-combustible fire in a peat bog.

For example, during the period between the end of World War II and the mid-1980s, much communication designed to sell something to an unwitting somebody gravitated toward two dissimilar poles.

Pole 1: raw description. Some unimaginative marketers, especially catalogers, actually believed readers would respond to what appeared to be utter candor.

Pole 2: unproved shouts of superiority. Other unimaginative marketers believed they could thump their chicken-skinny chests and proclaim, "We're the greatest!"—and both prospects and competitors would grovel.

What antediluvian attitudes! In those gentler times the term *marketer* included these primitives. But today's skeptical target sees an ad with the heading, "We'll Stand On Our Head to Please You," with a photograph of the store owner standing on his head—and thinks, "What a clown."

Today's marketing target ignores raw description and doesn't respond to strident hucksterism or unproved shouts of superiority. But this very skepticism gives force-communicators a competitive edge . . . if they know how to exploit that edge.

Many don't. Many still depend on bland description or chest-thumping. They're out of sync with the 1990s marketplace.

How do you get in sync? Wellll . . .

Depending on who you are and what you think of the notion of power communication you're either

> a. reading my words,
> b. skimming over my words,
> c. finally reading my actual words,
> d. noting my words,
> e. poring over my wisdom, or
> f. your choice of 38,000 other ways of describing the same action.

That's what power communication is—influencing the reader through word choice. Technical writers can describe; advertisers and their agencies don't need our talents for that. The ability to describe is just one of the components of the art (and even science, now that you have this book) of persuasion.

For example: Suppose I had written, two paragraphs back, ". . . 38,000 other ways of saying the same thing." Is this identical to ". . . 38,000 other ways of describing the same action"?

Yes, from the viewpoint of comprehension; no, from the viewpoint of persuasion. Why? Because the word *thing* is as nondescript as any word in the lexicon.

That's why the power communicator eschews clichés such as *quality* (which, through overuse, no longer has any quality), *value* (which has no value), and *service* (which suggests no specific). Yet we see advertising every day with headings—*headings*, for God's sake!—such as:

Where You'll Find Quality, Value, and Service

The dilettantes are invading our ranks!

(While our brains are momentarily open, consider another seldom-analyzed weakness—beginning a sales argument with the phrase "Where You'll Find.")

Separating Wheat from Chaff

I long have suggested an early-weeding procedure for employers and head-hunters to separate the chaff from writers with real power potential:

Give the prospects—and they're all whizzes at writing resumés—an opportunity to write some descriptive selling copy right there, in front of you or your personnel manager. Lard the information-sheet they're to use as background information with words such as *utilize, annual, requested,* and *commence.* While you're at it, use *for* when you mean *because.*

If the sample copy regurgitates those words back at you, pass. You have a writer to whom exciting the reader is secondary to projecting the writer's own image.

Mindless writing may have its place . . . for example, in technical manuals. Imaginative writing can damage descriptions whose effectiveness depends on their being dispassionate.

So a technical writer is blameless for telling us we get a "pint bottle." The journeyman writer gets some brownie-points for upgrading to "half-quart bottle"; but the force-communicator, whose professionalism results from the ability to shape the reader's plastic attitude, dares not miss the free shot: "tiny half-quart bottle" or "huge half-quart bottle."

Optimizing Information

Every paragraph of every chapter of this book explores ways to optimize information.

For example, now that we've made ourselves re-aware of the weakness of such words as *quality* and *service* and *value*, let's scout our territory for other wilting leaves. We all know the numeral 3 is more dynamic than *three*; we all know the writer *always* has a stronger way to begin a selling argument than the phrase "There is . . ." or "There are . . ."; we all know the individual whose copy is larded with *utilize* and *indeed* is skirting the edge of rapport instead of embracing it.

Ah, but *using* this argumentative edge eludes too many copywriters.

Word choice shouldn't be random. We're describing perfume. What does it have? A smell? An aroma? A scent? A fragrance?

Word use can't—or rather, shouldn't—be casual. That's why first-person writing should be congruent with an implicit decision: Is this to be a tight communication or a breezy one? Imperative or indicative? Maintaining the head of steam demands that the *mood* of the communication be consistent.

Now, what if the previous paragraph had ended with "Maintaining the head of steam suggests . . ." instead of "Maintaining the head of steam demands . . ."? No problem *if* the overall tone of

LENOX

Stephen M. Yanklowitz
President

Dear Collector,

There are certain images from the Bible that are so powerful, they serve as a constant affirmation of faith.

Jesus the Saviour portrays just such an image in a new and original sculpture from Lenox, created for your collection.

This fine work of art depicts a very important moment in Jesus' ministry. It is at The Last Supper when He has just spoken to His disciples of troubling events to come in the days that will follow. And then to comfort and inspire them, He assures them that He will find a place for them in His "father's house." And that all who believe will most assuredly find a place with Him.

Everything about this work of art conveys that message of redemption and salvation, portrayed with the extraordinary sensitivity and flawless detail reminiscent of the great Renaissance artists. Look at the steadfastness with which Jesus stands, His arms upraised in an inspiring gesture. And the peace and solemnity emanating from His face.

Superb Lenox sculpting also captures the intricate folds of His garment, and perfectly defines each finger of His hands, all in the pure white bone china that is ideal for the subject.

Like the other works in your Life of Christ Collection, this is a fine sculpture worthy to be an heirloom, a work to display in your home every day of the year. One that will be cherished in your family for as long as there are times in life that require hope and faith. For it will elevate...comfort ...and inspire.

Jesus the Saviour is available exclusively from Lenox. We have made it simple for you to bring this important work of art into your home now. Just return your reservation by the date it bears.

Sincerely,

Stephen M. Yanklowitz
President

SMY:mcd

LENOX COLLECTIONS, LANGHORNE, PENNSYLVANIA 19047

Fig. 1.1

"There are. . ." weakens the opening of this letter. Easier to read and more forceful, this alternative opening retains the exact message: "Certain images from the Bible are so powerful, they serve as a constant affirmation of faith."

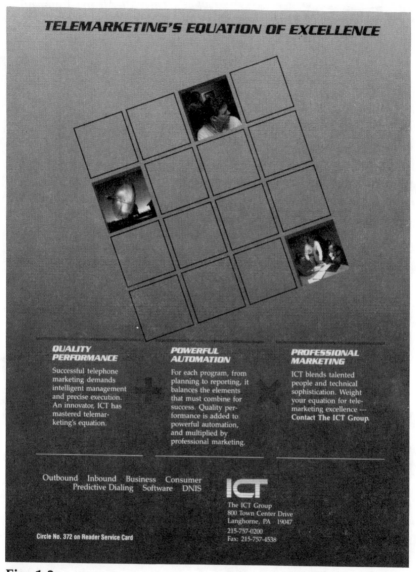

Fig. 1.2

Would you hire the copywriter who wrote this? Does this communication—in full color and full bleed—transmit any information to motivate the casual reader to contact the company? The company calls itself an innovator. In what way? What are "the elements that must combine for success"?

the communication had been advisory rather than commanding. But the very phrase "head of steam" is commanding. It demands *demands*.

The reader, viewer, or listener is like a rat in a maze. Our job is to prod that reader into the right direction.

Which brings us to the cornerstone of all communication that actually communicates, powerfully or not. . . .

The Clarity Commandment

The engine of any effective message is *clarity*. The floor under every message you speak or write has to be *The Clarity Commandment*:

> ■ In force-communication, clarity is paramount. Don't let any other component of the communications mix interfere with it.

I've pitched this Commandment at readers in half a dozen other books; if you're reading this one, it may be (and I hope it is) redundant.

Still, sometimes we become enraptured with the "game" of communicating. We want to outwit the reader or listener, and connection becomes secondary to showing off a big vocabulary or struggling to generate a "different" type of message. We violate the Clarity Commandment . . . and we pay for our sin by depressing response.

Remember the television show in which contestants faced a board displaying a bunch of magnetized letters? The contestant shuffled the letters until they formed a word.

Now visualize that board with words on it, not letters. These are the words:

BEFORE INFORMATION NEVER PUBLISHED

Scrambling against the clock, the contestant gets this sequence—

NEVER BEFORE PUBLISHED INFORMATION

—and yells, "I win!"

Okay, if yours is the mentality of a quiz-show contestant. Not okay if you're writing a message that's supposed to get people to respond, which is what the author of this sequence was doing. Why isn't it okay? Because word-flow isn't optimized. A simple word switch gives you—

INFORMATION NEVER PUBLISHED BEFORE

—and reader-penetration is a little easier.

The obvious admonition: Just because *you* understand your words, don't assume somebody who didn't write them will understand them.

Clarity, Argot, and Verisimilitude

When addressing your audience remember *The Rule of Jargon Conviviality:*

■ If you want to connect with your reader, on convivial terms, use local argot . . . unless verisimilitude demands otherwise.

A letter in a promotional package from a mailing service in France ends this way (copy here is unchanged from the original):

*We wish to inform your that we are in possession of
the telephone subscribers national service and that our
renting service is at your disposal.*

*If you wish to enquire about au this advantages, you
are invited to take part in one of our openday. You
just have to call to arrange an appointment.*

Good or bad?

In my opinion, *both*. American usage long since has abandoned arm's-length constructions such as "We wish to inform
you" and "If you wish to enquire." That's exactly why it's good
in this usage. The message obviously is either (a) from someone
for whom English is a second language or (b) from someone whose
mastery of writing is strong enough to cause us to think English
is a second language. That adds verisimilitude.

It's bad because I, for one, don't know what an "openday"
is. I'll ignore with a grin "your" instead of "you" and "au" slipped
in for some obscure Gallic reason. But I can't forgive "openday"
because even if this letter were from Sandusky I'd still feel the
writer is saying, "I know something you don't"—and that's poor
copywriting.

Without clarity, any message is at best only partially transmitted.

Remember Who Your Reader Is

We're selling books or records or videotapes or memberships.
Staring at our merciless screens, we see what we've written:

If you sign up for the program . . .

Boss/bos/*adj* DEFINITION: *The very best; stylish, admirable, exciting, excellent, first-rate.* EXAMPLE: *"Hendrix Jimi the wow good really is, Beatles cute plenty are and the of course, but T. Rex is boss truly boss"— Serendipity McLemore, review of T. Rex in Psychedelic Gushing about Rock, 1966.* SOURCE: *Dutch baas, the best. First recorded use, 1836; in use ever since; revived in mid-60s white suburban teen slang.* NOTES ON USAGE: *Used mostly with music ("Let's spin some boss golden oldies"— Humble Harve, KHJ, Los Angeles, 1966) and fashions ("That's a real boss hairnet"). After 1980, used only by those who wish to reveal that they are fortysomething. Oddly enough, the Dutch word baas also means "master," whence the English noun boss. The Dutch are obviously fond of their superiors.* SYNONYMS: *batting a thousand, the caterpillar's kimono, A-number-one, in the groove.*

Fig. 1.3

*This paper company has developed a new texture called "Groove."
To promote it, the creative team developed a psychedelic ad with
copy aimed at—whom? Some art directors may be influenced by the
hyper-hip copy. Others will react negatively based on the writer's
dogged avoidance of specifics.*

The writer who would have flunked the *utilize* test plows merrily ahead. What the heck—the reader will understand what she's supposed to do.

That's exactly what's wrong. Signing up for a program can seem to be too profound a commitment when blared from the keyboard halfway through a pitch. Instead of suggesting the permanence of an unretractable signature, how about:

If you decide to try out the program . . .

The writer might have written "participate in the program" instead of "try out the program" . . . except for two aspects:

1. *Participate* intellectualizes the sales argument, and we've known for years that emotion outsells intellect,
2. *Try out* tells the reader, "You're in command"; *participate* tells the reader, "We're in command."

Power communication is, then, a matter of word-choice . . . penetrating our target's own experiential background. Here's the value of power communication.

You've been named one of six vice-presidents of your organization. When someone asks what your title is, office clerk mentality dictates this answer: "I'm a vice-president of the company."

The journeyman power persuader knows better. He or she drops one word, which enhances image without changing facts: "I'm vice-president of the company."

The meistersinger power persuader doesn't drop the *a*; he replaces it, and this change optimizes the information: "I'm the vice-president of the company."

If you've been regarding the difference between *a* and *the* as a grammatical footnote, I suggest you change your thinking. In a competitive ambience, the other chap is a vice-president; you're *the* vice-president. (Chapter 4 explores the benefit of the definite article to establish exclusivity; it also explores the relationship between the definite and indefinite articles.)

We Know How to Write. Do We Know How to Sell?

Writers? Everybody and his brother can write. We're a plateau above. We're the elite. We're marketers.

Consider a primitive marketing example: You're selling green-tinted writing-paper. You want to imply superiority. You've settled on the heading, "Successor to [A WORD HERE] White Writing Paper."

On your own notepad is a listing of adjectival candidates. Which word would you use in your copy, to elevate your writing paper above its competition? In descending order, depending on how negative you want the competition to appear to be: "Successor to ☐ regular ☐ standard ☐ ordinary white paper." What if you really want to slam the competition? Then you'd use "old-fashioned."

Rats in a Maze

The purpose of this book is to splatter sunshine all over the rhetorical path to *dominance through word-choice*—the only way we, as communicators, can control "those people," readers and viewers of our messages, during the mid and late 1990s.

I'll explain.

In the brutally competitive "force-communication" ambience, the shrewd marketer scrutinizes verbiage. Why? Because words are the key to *Power Persuasion* and often the difference between a motivating and nonmotivating message.

Does attention to salesmanship, to primitive psychology, to unsophisticated techniques of opinion-making require a massive education in marketing? I certainly hope not. To the contrary. Overeducated marketers depend on overblown rhetoric and avoidance of our grubby, soiled-hand marketplace.

Quel dommage! (Sorry. How sad! See what happens when the writer shows off?) Their pocket calculators can transmit pure numbers . . . but not the sales they lose by their ignorance of the difference in impact between "Nearly half" and "less than half." For that matter, they can't consider—because they don't know—that "nearly half" is more than "almost half" but less than "practically half."

Look at our target-readers, viewers, and listeners as rats in a maze. They flounder. Great!

Our job is to push them through the maze. So we give them a piece of cheese here. We open a gate there. We touch them with an electric prod over there. The rats rush through the maze and out the exit. They go where we guide them.

Understand, please: Adding power to your rhetorical porridge has a singular goal—helping to get those rats through the maze. Neither the concept nor application of the concept is a comfortable cloak for the faint of heart . . . nor for those accountants and clerks who sometimes, bewildered and bewilderingly, find themselves dictating a company's or advertising agency's marketing philosophy.

Fig. 1.4

A weak idea feeds on itself. The concept of this ad is non-selling— starting with "There's . . ." compounds the problem by making an oblique pass at the selling argument instead of banging it head-on.

Those would-be's are marketing troglodytes. To have them dictating either creative philosophy or budget expenditure is criminal.

As our rhetorical juggernaut rushes toward the year 2001, we had better dig deep into our bag of stylistic tricks if we're to stay one step ahead of our ever-more-sophisticated readers, viewers, and listeners.

Invasion of the Phrase-Snatchers

Stop right there, please, if you're reading *viewpoint* into this interpretation. No! The difference gives us ammunition *both ways*. We can avoid subliminal irritation just as readily as we can stimulate it.

All right, then. What's the benefit to *us* of knowing (or even sensing) these differences?

It's the standard benefit of power communication: the ability to skew the reader's perception without changing the facts.

A disclaimer: This is fine for us; it's an unworthy weapon for supposedly dispassionate journalists who use Power Persuasion to bolster their preconceived opinions. I salute their astuteness . . . and damn their thin ethics, because *our* role is to persuade; *their* role is to inform.

In a marketing publication, I read a bylined news story—*not* intended to be an opinion piece—describing a racial boycott of an athletic shoe manufacturer. The reporter left no doubt where his sympathies lay: "A full 39% agreed that a company selling to minorities is obliged to return some of its profits to minority groups and hire minority advertising agencies."

Hold it! Suppose *you* were the reporter and you held an opposing view. Would a sense of ethics prevent you from writing,

"An overwhelming 61% disagreed with the concept that a company selling to minorities is obliged to return some of its profits to minority groups and hire minority advertising agencies"?

The facts aren't at fault. The reporter quoted a survey. Adjectival insertions do generate a reader reaction, especially if the reader has no preconceived opinion. Get rid of "A full" and "An overwhelming" and you have the facts, unskewed.

In an age of investigative reporting, compassion gives way to the writer's personality-projection. The line between editorial opinion and raw, untampered fact no longer exists . . . as witness this very comment!

I have to believe power communication parallels atomic energy. Like all forces for the good, it faces occasional corruption at the hands of the Hitlers and Husseins of communication. Corruption bends it but doesn't shatter its worthiness.

The Doublespeak Diversion

"Doublespeak" is the technique of trying to make bad news seem good, trying to make a lie seem true, trying to cloud the mind of someone who understood perfectly well what you said before.

Doublespeak *isn't* power communicating, and, in fact, gives the art of professional communication a bad name. Television comedians don't make derisive jokes about power communication; doublespeak is their lawful prey.

Doublespeak came to full flower under President George Bush, whose "Read my lips: No new taxes" became a harelip when taxes went up. But they didn't. They weren't new taxes; they were "revenue enhancements" and "user fees."

Speaking of enhancements, Chrysler Corporation offered some 5,000 employees a "career alternative enhancement program." In non-doublespeak, it meant they got pink slips. A municipal sanitary district had an "anomaly"—not an accident—resulting in "repositioned organic biomass." In nondoublespeak, this meant somebody accidentally released sewage sludge into the canal.

In the early 1990s doublespeak became such a national joke a book by that title (*Doublespeak*, by William Lutz) was a national best-seller.

Doublespeakers don't lie. They use "terminological inexactitude." But what they really do is cast a cloud over *all* communication, adding fuel to the Age of Skepticism. Don't join them. Deliberate miscommunication angles away from the authentic communicator's goal: The communicator doesn't want to generate secondary annoyance when people realize what the message really meant.

If you're a power communicator you have enough legitimate weapons without having to add the poison gas of that deadly first syllable to *mis*communication.

Synonyms Aren't Synonymous

A benefit the whole concept of power communication bestows is the expanding universe of communication to which we become privy. We begin to *think* in terms of information-optimizing . . . and we're less likely to excrete a self-canceling message.

Synonyms aren't always synonymous. Assumption of synonyms is a principal procreator of the less-than-effective message. We use perfectly acceptable "parallel" words, but they may not be the most effective words.

Our constant question, as force-communicators: *Are* these words generating the emotional reaction I intended, or have I mounted a fourteen-inch tire on a fifteen-inch rim—close, but unsafe rhetorical transportation?

Oh, copywriters who have become weary of using the word *beautiful* to describe a work of art may switch to *lovely* or *exquisite* without too much fear. The words are mildly parallel; they serve their purpose by sidestepping reader-boredom.

But other words *aren't* so easily switched.

Keep Your Weapon Sharp, Whoever You Are!

Fund-raising, a generally laudable enterprise, may well be the most logical avenue for power communication. Oddly, fund raisers have only partially recognized this mighty rhetorical mace. A fund raising mailing for one of the biggest charities for children (a lesser communicator might wreck the message right there by writing "biggest children's charities") had this key line:

At night she eats only a bowl of rice.

What's wrong with that, you ask? Your own experiential background is what's wrong. We order soup at a restaurant. The waiter asks, "Do you want a bowl or a cup?" We've learned that a bowl is *more* than a cup, so having her eat "only a bowl of rice" doesn't grab us the way "only a cup of rice" would. Had I written that message, I'd have pulled out even more stops:

Her only meal is a handful of rice.

If you're wondering about the ethical aspects of this change, ask yourself: Just what is the fund-raiser's job, anyway? We're hammering home: This child doesn't get enough to eat. Her bowl or cup probably in fact, does not hold more than a handful of rice. Our job is to transmit the message with the greatest penetration into the reader's apathy, generating as dramatic and dynamic a reaction as words can accomplish. And if you didn't know the difference between supposedly impartial reporting and power *persuasion*, you wouldn't be reading these words in the first place.

One more, for this chapter:

Add to your list of danger-words this apparently harmless candidate: *read*.

Why? *Read* is work. It requires education and time. So when your copy is pitched below the highest levels, or when reading isn't part of what you're selling, weigh the possibility of adding apparent reader comfort by a simple switch—instead of "Read what users say," we write, "Look at what users say."

Does changing a word here and there really add impact?

Even feathers, in bulk, can have noticeable weight. (Doesn't this have more impact than "In bulk, even feathers can have noticeable weight"? The reader's eye, hitting "bulk" before "feathers," knows too much too early. See how easy power communicating is?

Chapter 2
Power Communicating with Numbers and Punctuation Marks

A number is a number, right?

A pair of quotation marks just sets off a quotation or title, right?

Wrong . . . if you're a power communicator.

Let's first look at the power lurking in numbers: The stylebook says we spell out numbers from one through nine and use numerals for 10 or above.

We know better. For example, which of these is better? 3 or *Three*?

Yes, this example is easy. We know implicitly: If we want a dynamic message, we use the numeral 3. If we want sophisticated copy, we spell it out—T-H-R-E-E.

How many times have we seen an ad for an expensive dress, with the price spelled out . . . Eight hundred and fifty dollars.

("Eight hundred and ninety-nine dollars" has less verisimilitude. Why? Because the "ninety-nine," a too-common sale number, is out of key with the technique.)

The writer is fulfilling the power communicator's function altering the reader's perception without changing the facts.

The Rule of Numerical Manipulation

The power communicator uses numbers to manipulate the target individual's reaction. Converting a headline from "Family

Protection for $7.50 a Month" to "Is Your Family's Future Worth 25¢ a Day to You?" resulted in an exponential jump in response.

The reason wasn't a guilt/fear blend, the communicator's "huggy-blanket"; the original headline had primitive elements of those components. Rather, it was putting the numbers within absorbable reach. This sharpened and heightened guilt/fear and emphasized what the seller is supposed to emphasize: how easy it is.

The underlying rule is a two-way rule, *The Rule of Numerical Manipulation:*

■ Deciding whether to break numbers into component fragments or pile them into totals depends on whether you want your target to think he/she is spending money or getting money.

You don't have to pay a consultant to know individuals want to spend as little money as possible and bank as *much* money as possible. Which would you rather spend? 25¢ a day, $7.50 a month, or $90 a year? They're the same amount of money, but the psychological overtones aren't remotely parallel.

We'll explore an avenue that *is* parallel in a subsection later in this chapter, "The Generic Determination Rule."

Decimals or Fractions

If you want to present a number less than one in its most positive face, decimals seem bigger than fractions.

Suppose you're selling a mini-refrigerator. Would you write—

One-half cubic foot capacity?

or—

½-cubic foot capacity?

or—

.5 cubic foot capacity?

The power communicator probably votes for .5 cubic foot, because emphasis shifts to "cubic foot." Like most decimals, .5 is moderately obfuscatory. Unable to penetrate at first glance, the eye moves to the next item in line.

Please note: This point doesn't relate to the Generic Determination Rule, which accepts half a quart as a bigger quantity than one pint, 60 seconds as a shorter time than one minute, or 5280 feet as a shorter distance than one mile.

When to Avoid Using *No.* for *Number*

In a sweepstakes or any "yes/no" reply device, if you have a number, don't abbreviate the word *number—no*. Some readers will think "Entry no." means "No entry."

Don't laugh at this. Many people still cross out *No.* on blank checks and write in, "Yes." The Clarity Commandment has to reign supreme over all communication.

Plus vs. Minus

Which is stronger—

$$4 - 2 = 2?$$

or—

$$2 + 2 = 4?$$

Don't equate this with the ancient comparison of a pessimist ("The glass is half empty") with an optimist ("The glass is half full"). Subtraction can be stronger than addition when you want your target to realize that time's a-wastin'. If your approach is, "You're about to miss out," consider subtraction rather than addition.

This parallels the use of *more* and *less*. You generate different reactions by telling your target that others are, (a) *much more unsophisticated* . . . or (b) *much less sophisticated*.

The Generic Determination Rule

Obviously the difference between numerals and spelled-out numbers doesn't apply to the spoken word; but *The Generic Determination Rule* does:

- The generic determines reaction more than the number.

The Rule is simple enough: One gallon is a greater quantity than four quarts. A kilometer is a greater distance than 1000 meters. One mile is a greater distance than 5,280 feet. 5,280 feet is a greater distance than 5280 feet. Sixty minutes is less time than one hour.

Reaction is drawn more to the generic unit than to the number. This can be helpful in writing or saying, "We ship within

24 hours" to suggest a faster turnaround than "We ship within one day" . . . or, "Lease this car for 60 months," less time than "Lease this car for five years" . . . or, "No payments due for one full month," a longer no-payment time than "No payments due for 30 days."

Strings of Numbers vs. Fractions

A string of numbers appears to be a greater amount than a fraction. So when you want to imply greater quantity, use the string of numbers; when you want to imply lesser quantity, use fractions. We have *The Ballooning Number Rule:*

- The farther a number rises beyond the average individual's personal experiential background, the less emotion the number generates.

In practice, this means a reader or listener accepts a national debt figure of trillions of dollars *intellectually*; the same reader or listener accepts "This means *you* owe more than $20,000" *emotionally*. Target involvement calls for readily digestible numbers.

Don't be proud of the mathematician in you when you're writing to trigger an emotional reaction. This approach is clever, to the point, and inventive:

At just $22.98 that comes to just under $0.000006754 per taste bud!

Is it founded in fact? Let the skeptical reader disprove it. But the nine-digit decimal is impenetrable, which makes this an intellectualized slide-rule version of a winning idea. Let's see: .000 is

1/10¢. .0000 is 1/100¢. .00000 is 1/1000¢. So we might adapt this statistic to read—

For each 1¢ you'll tickle more than 1,500 taste buds!

or, more slavishly faithful to the original—

At just $22.98 that comes to more than 1500 taste buds for each penny.

Zeros Add the Impression of Size

In sweepstakes copy, use as many zeros as you can.

Zeros add the impression of size. So $1,000,000 is more money than $1 million. For that matter, $1,000,000.00 is more money than $1,000,000.

Primitive psychology is at work here. Let's have it help us whip up a head of steam.

The lower the number, the more valuable zeros become. So using them for $200—$200.00—is more significant than using them for $1,000,000. Why? Because the million dollars has six zeros. We're adding ⅓ more. $200 has two zeros. We're doubling the number.

This recommendation is for sweepstakes copy. High-fashion and top-of-the-line appeals should drop the zeros. At the very top it's "one million dollars," not "$1,000,000" or "$1 million."

$200 a Day? $6,000 a Month? $70,000 a Year?

Suppose you're advertising a part-time business opportunity. Which phraseology will sell your deal?

- Make an Extra $100 a Day!
- Make an Extra $3,000 a Month!
- Make an Extra $35,000 a Year!

Careful, now. This is the stuff tests are made of. We eliminate the month, not because of the amount but because it's neither here nor there: It doesn't have the immediacy of the day nor the dollar power of the year.

If we test "$100 a Day" against "$35,000 a Year" we should make a simple change to add some weight to the year. Instead of "Make an Extra $35,000 a year," emphasize a word which *aims* the interpretation in the direction we want it to go: "Make an *Extra* $35,000 a Year!"

Emphasizing the word *Extra* adds two separate kinds of impact—to the amount and to the *comparative* amount relative to the target-individual's existing income.

So a yearly total doesn't work as well when telling the reader an amount to pay . . . but it's worth testing when telling the reader how much he gets. Why isn't it an automatic assumption? Because the "Right now!" aspect of the day may or may not overpower the dollar total of the year.

The Subrule of Numerical Manipulation

Because this concept *isn't* automatic, we have *The Subrule of Numerical Manipulation:*

- If the total number gives greater greed satisfaction than the immediacy of the daily number, go with the total number.

The Subrule gives us the formula for choice among these five candidates:

- We'll send you a million dollars a year for life!
- We'll send you $1,000,000 a year for life!
- We'll send you $83,333 a month for life!
- We'll send you $19,000 a week for life!
- We'll send you $2,739 every day for life!

The amounts are the same. Some of the numbers are difficult for a brain to massage. So which of these headings is a better numerical manipulator?

We'll send you $2,739 every day for life!

or—

We'll send you $2,000 every day for life!

Purists might argue for $2,739. Nobody, they'll say, would invent a number like that. It has verisimilitude. It has to be true.

Salespeople, who know we need broader strokes for instant information assimilation, prefer $2,000. It's an easy number, a nonthreatening number, and—most significant when we're throwing assumptions at our targets—a number that doesn't have the reader or listener struggling to comprehend what it is. It's *comfortable* . . . so in this instance, less is more.

But can $2,000 a day compete with a million a year? Oh, no. The American Dream is to be a millionaire, not a "thousandaire," and the magic million-dollar number provides instant imagination gratification.

Now, why choose "a million dollars" instead of

Join the Prime Choice™ Program and take stock in a 750 million dollar industry.

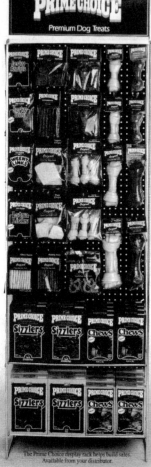

Introducing the Prime Choice Premium Dog Treat Program, the first and only complete line of dog treats sold exclusively in pet shops. With Prime Choice, you now have the opportunity to cash in on the extremely profitable dog treat market.

Every year, dog owners spend over $750 million on dog treats. Unfortunately, they spend almost none of it in pet shops. In fact, last year pet shops sold only 2% of the tremendous jerky and biscuit categories.

But now, just as pet shops have captured a surprising $500 million in pet food sales from supermarkets, Prime Choice lets you get your share of the highly lucrative dog treat business.

Prime Choice has selected only the 27 best-selling dog treat items, including 100% nutritionally complete biscuits, high-protein jerky treats, and tartar-control beefhide (plain and basted).

We then created vivid, premium-quality packaging and a convenient, eye catching display system to entice your customers and drive impulse purchases.

The result is a unique, total program that's guaranteed to help build your business. To find out more about the new Prime Choice Program, contact your local distributor or call Dave Horton at 1-800-876-2885.

The Prime Choice display rack helps build sales. Available from your distributor.

Fig. 2.1

Would this ad have been more dynamic if the headline had used the number "$750,000,000" instead of "750 million dollars"? Note that within the text, the writer switches to "$750 million." The dollar sign is a dependable eye-grabber, and the headline should have taken advantage of it.

"$1,000,000.00" or "$1 million"? The spelled-out number *in this instance* has impact because the brain seizes each word individually.

How about "a million" instead of "one million"? The answer depends on the ambience. Most people respond more favorably to the informal than to the formal, which makes "a million dollars" preferable unless the words are individually accented: *one million dollars.* (One million, in a comparative listing, does seem to be more than a million. More on *one* versus *a* in chapter 4.)

A footnote to all this: It's "a million dollars a year," not "a million dollars per year." *Per* is an accountant's explanation, and accountants are poor salespeople.

Statistics Don't Sell

Good fund-raising writers know something lousy fund-raising writers don't know—*The Rule of Statistical Deficiency*:

- Readers respond less to cold-blooded statistics than they do to warm-blooded examples.

So instead of writing—

75% of the children afflicted with this terrible ailment might be saved.

they'll write—

Of four afflicted children who died, three of them might have been saved.

A more accomplished writer would guide the reader's interpretation by switching from passive to active and/or italicizing the key word—

> *Of four afflicted children who died, we might have saved* three of them.

But really, we're still dealing in statistics. Oh, sure, three out of four is more humanized than 75%. But a fund-raiser who knows his or her craft recognizes the Rule of Statistical Deficiency and projects the message in a framework aimed squarely at the empathic response of the reader or listener—

> *We lost Jimmy today. For months his bright eyes were filled with pain. Now they're closed forever. All his parents' hopes and dreams are shattered. But Nancy, Erin, and Billy still may have a chance to lead normal, healthy lives . . .*

The domination actual numbers have over percentages is just as pronounced in commercial messages. Look at the colossal difference between these two parallel notices:

> *We pay a broker's commission of 6%. But if you sell this house for $200,000 within the next month, we'll give you a bonus of an extra 1%.*

or—

> *We pay a broker's commission of 6%. But if you sell this house for $200,000 within the next month, we'll give you a bonus of $2,000.*

When TRW and 25,000 other corporations need to house their employees temporarily for special assignments, training or relocation, they use Oakwood Corporate Apartments. For an average of $52 a night, half the cost of a hotel room, they receive a full sized apartment, fully furnished with all the comforts of home. Plus the recreational amenities of a resort: swimming pools, spas, tennis and fitness centers. In 50 locations in business centers across the country, Oakwood Apartments is the choice of 300 of the Fortune 500 for cost, comfort and convenience.

You could spend more...but why settle for less?

"I spent 32 weeks out of town on special assignment last year and saved $6,600 in hotel bills!"

Oakwood ℠
Corporate Apartments
The Un-Hotel℠
Half the cost of hotels.
Twice the space and comfort.

Fig. 2.2

Would this message have been as effective if the wording had been "I spent more than 60% of the weeks out of town on special assignment last year and saved 42% in hotel bills"? Percentages are more intellectualized than actual numbers and, except for very small numbers, have less impact.

Analysis gives us *The Rule of Percentile Feebleness*:

- Unless the numerical amounts are tiny, actual numbers have greater impact than percentages.

Don't mistake the Rule to mean "0%" has power. We see this in automobile ads, but seeing it doesn't justify it. "0% Financing" is weaker than "No Finance Charges" because the percent is arm's-length and attention is to the *concept* of percent. The message recipient's absorption of 0 is tempered by % and *Financing*.

No isn't usually a good opener, but here, emphasis on the negative is what the communicator is after. "No Finance Charges" is in turn weaker than "Never a Finance Charge." "You Don't Pay One Cent of Finance Charges" is another step up; "You Don't Pay Even One Cent of Finance Charges" is an extra half-step. Much as we all love positives and the word *free*, "Free of Finance Charges" is confusing and may lead to ill will.

Give Numbers "Breathing Room"

Give each significant number or statistic "breathing room" or it loses impact from the proximity of other numbers—which also lose impact.

Let's suppose we have a long-distance service. Our sponsored research project gives us a promotionally usable statistic: 60% prefer our service to AT&T.

We use this in our sales letter (and we use it properly: instead of the cold-blooded "60%" we warm it up by writing "3 out of 5").

$0

AmTrust Bank Home Equity Lines for people in the no.

Did you know that, as of January 1,1991, one of the only interest deductions allowed by law is the interest you pay on your home? That means, with our Home Equity Line you'll get a tax break plus:

No **application fee!**

No **points!**

No **closing costs!** We will waive all closing costs if you borrow $5000 or more at closing.

No **principal payments!** You are only required to pay interest as low as 1% over the Wall Street Journal prime rate. This means you'll have the lowest possible monthly payments.

Nothing is more convenient! To give yourself a loan, simply write a check, any day, any time, for any reason.

AmTrust Bank
A Savings Bank

BOCA RATON	MISSION BAY	CORAL SPRINGS
1850 N. Federal Hwy.	10101 Glades Rd.	707 University Dr.
Joanne Ballway	Bob Thomas	Cathy Albamonte
(407) 368-9600	(407) 483-2517	(305) 345-5227

If you make no principal payments, you may have to refinance your line or have a balloon payment at the end of your 15 year loan term. Your interest rate cannot exceed 16%. The Wall Street Journal prime rate as of 5 2 91 is 8.5%. Consult your tax advisor regarding deductibility of interest

EQUAL HOUSING LENDER

Fig. 2.3
Financial institutions gravitate toward zeroes. But a zero used alone always requires an explanation and re-evaluation. Doesn't the Am-Trust Bank ad headline suggest this bank has no money for home equity loans?

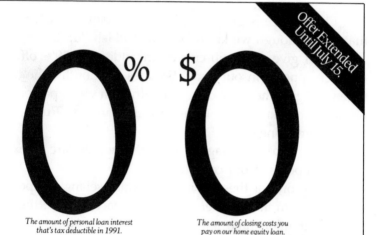

0% $0

The amount of personal loan interest that's tax deductible in 1991.

The amount of closing costs you pay on our home equity loan.

Two Reasons For Getting A Barnett Home Equity Loan That Have Nothing In Common.

As many of you probably already know, the tax laws have changed. And as of January 1991, the interest on most personal loans is no longer deductible.

Just about the only personal interest that is deductible is that which you pay on your home.*

That's where a Barnett Home Equity Loan comes in. Not only do you get a loan with tax deductibility, you also get one

that's very flexible. You can use it to pay for a car, a boat, a vacation or tuition.

You can even use the funds to make certain investments or consolidate other loans into just one payment.

That's not all. Now through July 15, Barnett will pay the closing costs associated with the loan.** That can save you hundreds of dollars right from the start.

To make things easier, have your loan

payment automatically deducted from your checking or savings account. For recurring borrowing needs, ask about Barnett's Home Equity CreditLine.

To receive a Home Equity Loan application by mail, call 1-800-825-6800 or personally pick one up at your local Barnett office. See how a couple of things that have nothing in common can actually save you money.

*Subject to certain important qualifications, generally, interest paid on home secured loans is tax deductible. Please consult with your individual tax advisor for the tax consequences of any Barnett loan.
**Offer applies only to Home Equity Loans. Normal closing costs apply to other mortgage finance programs. Offer expires July 15, 1991. All Barnett Banks are insured by the FDIC. ©1991 Barnett Banks, Inc.

 **Barnett Bank** Florida's Bank. Since 1877.

Our service is priced "up to" 35% below AT&T. So we use that, even though we know how weasel-ish "up to" is.

We'll give new subscribers an additional 10% off. So this number appears in our copy. So does 12 months, the length of time we'll give them the discount (although we as power communicators now know the Generic Determination Rule: "one full year" seems longer).

But to take advantage of this offer, we declare an expiration date. It appears in our copy too.

Every one of these points is a valid selling weapon. But if we pack them all together, we lose impact because the reader's relative attention ratio is split among them. None of them can claim major emphasis in this copy-block:

> *To get the long distance phone company 3 out of 5 preferred over AT&T at savings of up to 35% and our* Charter Customer Discount worth an additional 10% off your bill for 12 months, *you must sign and return the enclosed authorization form by October 31, 1992.*

If we want to expand our objections beyond number-clutter, we'd ask: "3 out of 5 *what?*"; and we'd wonder why the writer underlined so many words, reducing the power underlining can add. But we're on a subject more important than the logic of competitive long-distance carrier offers.

When and How Much to Underline

The novelist J.D. Salinger perfected a technique which pre-existed him but hadn't been widely used—underlining or italiciz-

Great Savings

30% to 50% off

(original price*)

women's and men's
shoes, ready-to-wear
and accessories

*Intermediate reductions may have been taken.

CHARLES JOURDAN
Paris

Miami: Bal Harbour Shops (305) 864-0621

Fig. 2.4
*Chopping 30 percent to 50 percent off original prices may truly be
"Great Savings," but wouldn't this flat announcement-advertisement
have been stronger with specific examples?*

ing to force the reader to follow the writer's intended emphasis. Easy to illustrate, using the same sentence: J.D. Salinger perfected a technique which pre-existed him but hadn't been widely used underlining or italicizing to *force* the reader to follow the writer's intended emphasis.

In the more formal world of salesmanship, some writers think using italics is garish. Opinion: They're wrong *if* (notice the italics forcing you to add emphasis to "if") adding accents also adds clarity. Clarity is the fuel making power communication possible.

A double caution:

1. Don't overuse italics.
2. Don't italicize a whole string of words when only one or two of them would make the point.

Both cautions are congruent with one of the Great Laws of force-communication: $E^2 = 0$ (when you emphasize everything, you emphasize nothing).

The easiest way to make the italic-determination is to read your communication aloud. Wherever your voice strengthens or rises, put a dot on the word or phrase. Then decide where to underline or italicize, as you'd decide how many ways you can change emphasis and listener perception when verbalizing statements such as—

- This is the first time we've opened our doors to the public.
- Even a dealer can't match your direct price.
- This outfit is very expensive-looking.
- The gift is yours free, no matter what you decide.

Consider the underline/italics principle as an automatic

option under two circumstances: (a) When a word/phrase or its opposite is repeated within a sentence; (b) when the word/phrase itself has an emotional potential.

These points are easy enough to illustrate. All we do to have a sample of A is repeat a sentence from a few paragraphs ago:

> *When you emphasize* everything, *you emphasize* nothing.

"Everything" and "nothing" are opposites, shown in opposition. Which gives us a simple sample of B:

> *"Everything" and "nothing" are opposites,* shown in opposition.

We've all used italics for years. Because so many writers overuse italics and so many others don't use them at all, isn't it time to figure out why?

Or, for complicity with this section, isn't it time to figure out *why*?

The Power in Quotation Marks

Do you know *The Quotation Mark Rule?*

- Putting quotation marks around a word or phrase the reader may not recognize tells the reader we share the novelty of the idea . . . and helps him or her accept the unknown. Without the quotation marks, we say to the reader, "We know something you don't."

Careful reading of this Rule will highlight the limitation:

"around a word or phrase the reader may not recognize." So the mailer whose copy referred to—

> . . . *the benefit of this "Crime Detector Program"*

missed the limitation. Better:

> . . . *the benefit of this "Crime Detector" Program*

The difference is in the intended interpretation. Putting quotes around "Crime Detector" emphasizes the two words as the *type* of program; including "Program" genericizes the emphasis, weakening the use of quotation marks.

Another example:

> *Special thermal paper gives you a bright, sharp image.*

The statement may be a mystery to those who associate the word *thermal* with heat. So a pair of quotation marks tells the reader the paper isn't really hot:

> *Special "thermal" paper gives you a bright, sharp image.*

Another, totally different but equally valuable use of quotation marks in power communication: Quotation marks are effective for generating a pejorative effect. An easy example:

> *This discount store supposedly has low prices.*

The statement presents information without prejudice either way; The word "supposedly" depends on reader interpretation

Fig. 2.5

Putting "The Professional's Source" into quotation marks changes the reader's perception from raw, unbacked puffery to outside opinion. Quotation marks are underused as power communications weaponry.

Fig. 2.6
Is "Dead End" too familiar a phrase to warrant implementation of the Quotation Mark Rule? Probably . . . but the quotation marks don't hurt and might actually attract an eye that otherwise would bypass the ad.

for a positive or negative effect. Adding a set of quotation marks clarifies the writer's intention . . . and the quotation marks aren't for the word "supposedly":

This "discount store" supposedly has low prices.

Now the message is clearly negative. The quotation marks suggest the store *doesn't* have low prices.

This use of quotation marks is a pleasant tool for political campaigns, for fund raisers using anger as a motivator, and for tough-minded comparisons:

- My "honest" opponent made some strange bank deposits.
- Unlike those other "non-profit" organizations, we use every cent to help our less fortunate brethren.
- So-called "long range" cordless phones have a range of 1,000 feet. Even our budget model has a range of 1,500 feet.

- "Budget" cellular phones cost $125 to $150. The Excel costs just $89.95.

Warning: Don't overuse quotation marks. *The Rule of Overuse* applies to all mechanical devices:

- Overuse = Abuse.

Parentheses to Suggest Exclusivity

Use parentheses to suggest exclusivity. Suppose you price your limited edition product at $100. The typical copywriter would write, "Price just $100." A more-aware copywriter would write, "Issue price just $100." A copywriter aware of motivational techniques would write, "Holiday House original issue price just $100." A power persuader writes:

Original issue price for preferred Holiday House collectors
$100

Adding parentheses appends a free exclusivity-booster:

Original issue price (for preferred Holiday House collectors)
$100

The parentheses are an implication: This price is *only* for preferred Holiday House collectors. Without the parentheses, the implication lapses into more obvious puffery.

Parentheses as Asterisk Replacements and De-Emphasizers

In an earlier book this author solved the enigma of when to use asterisks in power communication: *never*. Asterisks generate two reasons for communicator contempt.

One, asterisks too often indicate *exceptions*. We see an airline advertisement crowing about low fares. Oops! An asterisk!

Even before we look, we know the asterisk represents exceptions. What the airline giveth, the airline taketh away. One asterisk tells us the fare isn't valid during blackout periods (1 January to 31 December); another tells us the fare only applies if we stay over a weekend. A third tells us the fare doesn't apply to flights into and out of New York, Chicago, Los Angeles, Atlanta, Dallas, Miami, and Seattle. My point: The reader not only isn't surprised by the negatives implicit in the asterisk; years of asterisk reversals provoke that reader to approach the asterisk with a *negative* attitude.

Two, asterisks slow down both reading and comprehension. We come to a complete stop, because the asterisk drags our eye to the bottom of the page. Reading the inconsequential footnote—and it *has to be* inconsequential or it wouldn't be demoted to footnote purgatory—we lose pace. Rather, whoever made this rhetorical mistake loses pace for us.

A simple cure: Replace asterisks with parentheses. Suppose we have this statement:

*Examples of Low Fares**

The asterisk tells us:

**Not valid during blackout periods.*

The construction couldn't be more wrong. We've *doubled* attention to what we tried to throw away. So without changing even one word we replace this fumble with parentheses:

Examples of Low Fares (not valid during blackout periods)

The eye slides past the negative as we intended. (Yes, an accomplished wordsmith wouldn't have painted himself/herself into a "not valid" word-corner.)

The previous sentence employed another use of parentheses, first cousin of the asterisk replacement:

Use parentheses to de-*emphasize a point.*

"We aren't asking you for co-op money, as we sometimes have to do" has two components of equal weight; "We aren't asking you for co-op money (as we sometimes have to do)" apparently subordinates the second thought without actually doing so. Another example: "Using parentheses apparently subordinates the second thought (without actually doing so)."

Parentheses to Replace *Such As*

Replace *such as* with parentheses for smoothness in read-through comfort. Parentheses aren't a stop signal because they guide the reader's attitude sideways instead of directly forward, eliminating the possibility of a stop and backup for comprehension. **Example:**

Any disk operation, such as reading a directory, which doesn't specify a drive, appears on the current drive.

or—

Any disk operation (such as reading a directory) which doesn't specify a drive appears on the current drive.

A serendipitous by-product of the parenthetical substitution: Read-retarding commas aren't necessary.

Parentheses to Keep Your Target Smiling

An offbeat application of the parentheses—one to be used delicately and seldom:

Use parentheses to say to the reader when using a potentially destructive word: "I'm only kidding."

An easy negative/positive litmus test is the question, "Will the word erase a smile on your message recipient's face . . . or even cause it to waver?" A qualifier—in parentheses—holds the message in a positive channel.

Example: The serious word *Serious.*

In conversation, a chuckle can make this word positive. In writing, only the insertion of a parenthetical disclaimer such as "I'm (chuckle) serious" keeps the smile in place. A dangerous game, but one worth knowing about!

Replacing Commas with "And"

A series gains strength by replacing commas with "and": Instead of "A riot of colors—reds, greens, blues, purples, yellows," write, "A riot of colors—reds and greens and blues and purples and yellows." CAUTION: Use this sparingly, because it becomes "cutesy"-cloying in repetition.

Replacing Periods with "And"

Linking two thoughts with "and" instead of separating them with a period ties them together and by tying them splits the impact, making each component somewhat weaker: "You've been a loyal member, and we offer you this reward" . . . or, "You've been a loyal member. We offer you this reward."

This is one of those points usable both ways, similar to replacing commas with *and*. You may or may not want to de-emphasize one component by hitching it to another.

The Pros and Cons of Abbreviations

Spelling out abbreviated names *Mount Everest* instead of *Mt. Everest*, *Fort Lauderdale* instead of *Ft. Lauderdale*, *Street* and *Avenue* instead of *St.* and *Ave.*—adds dignity.

The power communicator can't use this for seldom-spelled contractions such as *Mr.* or *St.* in St. Louis, but can for Saint Christopher.

What about abbreviations for states—NY, VT, and the like?

If you want to obscure your location, use state abbreviations—IL, MA, IN. If you want to exploit your location, spell out the state—California, Ohio, Florida. For a "Good ol' boy" image, always spell out the state—Arkansas, Texas, Alabama. Don't intermix conviviality with technology.

Less Is More in Exclamation Points

Two exclamation points are weaker than one. "At last!!" suggests the writer is unsure of his/her ability to convince the reader. "At last!" is an exclamation that doesn't have the reader thinking, "The writer wants me to know this is an exclamation."

Dash, Ellipsis, or Comma?

Consider using dashes and ellipses when you sense an overuse of commas. (Parentheses also work as comma replacements.)

A dash ("—") is stronger than an ellipsis (". . ."), but that doesn't mean you should always use a dash. Sometimes you want a softer transition.

This is especially true when you *don't* want to call attention to whatever you've offset by dashes. A financial institution ran a newspaper ad with this as the first three sentences of body copy:

- If rates rise, our Ultimate Option CD lets you jump to a higher-rate CD without penalty—after the first year.
- It lets you withdraw your money for any reason without penalty—after the second year.
- If rates drop, it provides a three-year rate guarantee—to keep earnings high.

Did the writer really want to call attention to the first and second year exclusion of benefits? Suppose this same message had used commas? The *words* would be identical; *emphasis* would shift away from the exclusions:

- If rates rise, our Ultimate Option CD lets you jump to a higher-rate CD without penalty, after the first year.
- It lets you withdraw your money for any reason without penalty, after the second year.
- If rates drop, it provides a three-year rate guarantee to keep earnings high.

That third element could retain a dash, because the sales argument does want to call attention to *this* phrase; but a neatness complex (which usually weakens impact) probably would dictate parallel punctuation.

The ellipsis has no place in this type of construction.

Two additional choices regarding commas:

1. A colon at the end of a greeting is crisp and businesslike. A comma is casual and personal.
2. Omitting the comma from a number (2500 vs. 2,500) makes that number seem lower—and more convivial.

Use Hyphens When a Word is a Noun AND an Adjective

When an adjective is also a noun, you can gain an automatic increase in clarity by hyphenating. "Your attractive counter display..." isn't as instantly clear as "Your attractive counter-display."

NOVATRON
HUNT'S HAS IT ALL!!!
SELECT FROM OUR HUGE INVENTORY

novatron

Pro and Fun Kits
K-152C Fun Kit	$351.20
K-242C Fun Kit	391.20
60-150-2C Fun Kit w/Case	399.20
60-240-2C Fun Kit w/Case	439.20
61-500-3C Kit	831.20
61-600-3C Kit	959.20
68-1000-3C Kit	1183.20
68-1600-3C Kit	1303.20
68-1640-3C Kit	1327.20

Power Packs
Model 150 Pack	$136.00
Model 240 Pack	188.00
Model 300 Pack	236.00
Model 500 Pack	296.00
Model 600 Pack	388.00
Model 1000 Pack	540.00
Model 1600 Pack	680.00

500 W/S Heads CC
2000C Std. Head-15' Cable	$100.00
2005C Std. Head-25' Cable	104.00
2010C One Stop Head	120.00
2020C Two Stop Head	120.00
2030C New Bare Tube Head	140.00
*2060 16" Soft Head	140.00

1000 W/S Heads CC
2100C Std. Head-15' Cable	$108.00
2105C Std. Head-25' Cable	112.00
2110C One Stop Head	128.00
2120C Two Stop Head	128.00
2130C New Bare Tube Head	148.00
2133C 3-way BareTube Head	156.00
2140C 3-way Reduce Head	140.00
2142C Dual Head	232.00
2144C Quad Head	332.00
*2160 16" Soft Head	148.00

*Non CC Only

2630-FC1600w/s Fan Cooled Bare Tube Head - CC	$208.00

Monolights CC
200MC Mono Light 200 W/S	$228.00
400MC Mono Light 400 W/S	312.00
120M-SC Mono Light	168.00
240M-SC Mono Light	228.00

Accessories
Heavy Duty AC Power Cord	$6.00
AC Power Cord	4.80
15' Sync Cord	9.60
6101 Carrying Case	140.00
6801 Large Case w/Casters	188.00
4015 15' Extension Cable	32.00
4025 25' Extension Cable	36.00
5000 4' Back Light Stand	37.60
5008 8' Light Stand	36.80
5010 10' Light Stand	41.60
5020 Hvy. Duty Light Stand	92.00
Novatron Umbrellas	CALL
2032 6" Reflector-90	24.00
2034 16" Reflector-100	36.00
4000-A Snoot	26.40
4000-A1 Grid for Snoot	12.00
4001-A Adjustable Snoot	39.20
4001-A1 Grid Adj. Snoot	12.00
4005 Honeycomb Grid	32.00
4520 Grid w/Gel Holder	39.20
4010-A 2-Way Barn Doors	43.20
4011-A 4-Way Barn Doors	55.60
4020-A Diff/Gel Holder	23.20
4021 Diff/Gel Kit	23.96
4030 Slave	17.60

ASK FOR PAUL OR JOHN IN THE MAIL ORDER DEPT.
W.B. HUNT CO., INC.
100 MAIN ST.
MELROSE, MA 02176
(617) 662-6685
SEND FOR A FREE MAIL ORDER CATALOG!

Fig. 2.7

What effect do the three exclamation points have on the line "Hunt's has it all"? The impression is one of desperation, not exclamation. One exclamation point is stronger than two and, in extremis, two are better than three. Exclamatory multiples are more acceptable in "schlock" ads whose intention is to scream. But in an orderly presentation, they damage image.

Ampersands, *Et Cetera*, Et Al

Don't use ampersands except as a direct replication of a corporate logo. Don't use *etc.* under any circumstances: The word suggests others exist but you either (a) don't know what they are or (b) admit they're unimportant.

Writers often ignore numbers and punctuation as cornerstones of effective communication. These can be the key to clarity. Ignorance certainly *isn't* bliss, for writer or reader.

Chapter 3
Little Words Mean a Lot

Have we struck a mother lode when we realize that effective communication describes an electronic instrument as "miniaturized" instead of "small"? Is our attitude simplistic when we gauge the personality of someone answering the question we just posed, by the difference between the response "perhaps" and the response "maybe"? For that matter, are we picking nits when we make a conscious determination of the word *someone* instead of *somebody*, based on who our target-reader is? (See "Somebody Special," chapter 7.)

The answer to all three questions: *yes*. (A power communicator can intensify or diminish: a thundering yes; a definite yes; a thoughtful yes; a quiet yes.)

Synonyms Aren't Automatic Replacements

Synonyms aren't automatically interchangeable. Words exist because they're subtly different from other words whose meanings are *almost* the same. Often the differences are slight enough to make words interchangeable. (Example: The previous statement could have been, "Often the differences are minor enough . . ." or "so trifling . . ." or "so insignificant . . .")

In force-communication, slight or trifling or insignificant differences become substantial or consequential or significant if they modify the reader's reaction by a fraction of a percent. The effect parallels a ship heading for a harbor 500 miles away, using dead reckoning because weather prevents a clear view. A miscalculation of one degree means missing the harbor by miles.

Example: The difference between "immediately," "at once," and "right now." "At once" is the most imperative; "right now" is the most urgent; "immediately" is the most arm's-length.

What's the value of considering the difference of the three terms? "Immediately" is valuable when you don't want the message recipient to think you're assuming he or she will perform an action automatically. "At once" carries an imperious tone. "Right now" is a hard call to action.

The Biggest Little Word: *You*

Look for ways to inject *you* into the word mix. An insurance company's mailing had this as a key piece of copy:

> *We value your trust and confidence, and that is why we have worked so hard to make this unique coverage possible.*

We have a not-terrible, not-strong string of words. If the writer were a power communicator, we might have had:

> *We value your trust and confidence, and that is why we have worked so hard to make this unique coverage possible for you.*

The final two words tie the benefit to the target individual, just as the opening tied the premise to the target individual. Cost in creative time? Zero. Increase effectiveness? You name the percent.

When and *If*

When is better than *If* for suggesting something will happen. *If* is better than *When* for suggesting something won't happen.

This can be valuable when (not if) you're writing fund-raising copy, insurance copy, or any communication suggesting the possibility of a catastrophe, disaster, or unpleasant change.

For example—

When you have a claim . . .

is superior, when describing what a policyholder might expect from you, to:

If you have a claim . . .

But if you're selling cars, you don't want to suggest the possibility of a catastrophe, disaster, or unpleasant change. So you'd write or say:

If you ever see a rust-spot . . .

(Actually, you'd pull out all the stops: "In the unlikely event you ever see a rust spot. . . ." But that doesn't illustrate the difference between *when* and *if*.)

Adding Conditionality to the *When/If* Mix

Since *if* is conditional, adding a subjunctive to it increases the conditionality and softens the effect.

Fig. 3.1
The power communicator knows an "if" condition leaves the yes/no decision to the message-recipient; a "when" condition makes this decision for the message recipient. So the power communicator would have worded this: "When you want to buy or sell a car. . . ." The word "if" does have great value, however, when the writer wants to suggest a condition of equal yes/no possibility.

When you think credit card processing, think Litleprocessing℠

Litleprocessing™ is the credit card processing service of Litle & Co.

Litle & Co., 54 Stiles Road, Salem, New Hampshire 03079 Tel: 603-893-9333

For more information, circle No. 25

Fig. 3.2
In business-to-business advertising, "When" usually is a better opener than "If." Why? Because the advertiser assumes most readers have the capability of buying, and creating the buying assumption dictates "When," not "If."

"If you billed us once a month" is more straightforward—and therefore less conditional—and therefore harder—than "If you were to bill us once a month."

Inspect messages to determine how much conditionality you want to inject.

Adding *should* to the conditional mix gives us an extra dimension of weakness. "Should your policy ever be canceled" suggests less likelihood of cancellation than "If your policy is ever canceled." Adding *if* to *should* is median ground: "If your policy should ever be canceled. . . ." It isn't as likely to happen as *if* or as unlikely as *should*.

But the *if-should* combination isn't power communication. The power communicator makes a decision: The target is supposed to react positively or negatively . . . no shades of gray.

Why? Because we don't want to shift levels of interpretation into the hands of the message recipient. The palms on the rhetorical steering wheel have to be ours . . . and they shouldn't be sweaty with uncertainty.

Should takes a step oblique to direct involvement. This means "Do you want me to [WHATEVER]?" is stronger than "Should I [WHATEVER]?" You/me is unmistakably direct involvement between two parties; *should* puts the second party into a once-removed, mass-opinion position.

The "If" Challenge—Proceed with Caution

Be careful with "If . . ." challenges coupled with *would* or *should* or *could*.

In the subjunctive, an "if" challenge can suggest a condescending attitude toward the reader:

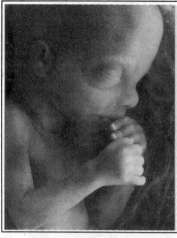

IF HE WERE BORN PREMATURELY, HE'D SURVIVE. BUT WOULD HIS HEALTH CARE PLAN?

Thanks to medical technology, babies now routinely survive the trauma of premature birth.

But there's a price to pay. Anywhere from $20,000 to $400,000 per baby. And increasingly, businesses are footing the bill as much as insurance carriers.

That's why you should consider the Baby Benefits program. By identifying as well as educating high risk mothers, it does what technology can't do.

Which is to help prevent premature births from happening in the first place.

For more information, please call (804) 354-4104.

Benefits That Deliver Before You Do.

CIRCLE NO. 29

Fig. 3.3

"If" instantly creates a condition. Would this message have been stronger with a "when" opening, that eliminates the soft "Would . . ."? Example: "He'll Be Born Prematurely. He'll Survive. But Will His Health Care Plan?"

WILLIAM K. WITCHER
2121 Precinct Line Road
Hurst, Texas 76054

IF YOU'RE SELF-EMPLOYED

this letter is of critical concern to you and you'll understand the importance of what we have to say.

H. G. Lewis
P.O. Box 12345
Anytown, USA 54321–0001

933-496-496   10753   5

If you're NOT self-employed, this is not for you.

Fig. 3.4

By creating a condition, the word "If" qualifies the reader. Assuming the typical recipient of this mailing is self-employed, this use of "If" suggests exclusivity—one of the great motivators of the 1990s.

WHEN IT COMES TO THEMES, WE'RE TRULY GIFTED.

Fig. 3.5

"When it comes to . . ." is implicitly weak and too obviously self-congratulatory. How would you reword this heading to replace this punchless heading?

If you were the publications director for a college or university, I wouldn't have to tell you who we are. You'd know us, because we print for more colleges than any other printer in America.

A change to present tense eliminates the danger:

If you're the publications director for a college or university, I don't have to tell you who we are. You know us, because we print for more colleges than any other printer in America.

"When It Comes To . . .": Ugh.

Even though "When" is superior to "If" for suggesting something will happen, "When it comes to . . ." joins "There is" and "It is" as a weak opening; in fact, "When it comes to . . ." outranks the other two because the very construction is *half* a parallel.

I'm looking at a full-page space ad headed, "When it comes to awards . . . *[a listing of six awards]* you've got to hand it to TIME."

Common enough; the reader doesn't flinch. But does flinching outrank yawning? The copy is punchless, not only because the concept is a cliché but also because the first half of the headline makes the second half apparent before we read it. It parallels superimposing "The butler did it" onto a key scene in a mystery movie.

When and *As Soon As*

When isn't as dynamic as *As soon as.*

Why? Because *When* has no personality and *As soon as* does: It makes the promise of immediacy.

Which is the more motivational sentence?

- When your referral deposit comes in, we'll credit your account an additional $5.00.
- As soon as your referral deposit comes in, we'll credit your account an additional $5.00.

As soon as yanks the statement out of the gray limbo of "maybe it'll happen and maybe it won't." We've replaced a nonselling word with a selling word, avoiding the tar pit of obvious hucksterism.

Should . . . . Had Better . . . Ought To

Had better is a more imperious imperative than *should*. *Ought to* is a stronger coax than *should*.

"We had better take care of this" means we have little choice; the alternative is unpleasant . . . an implied threat. "We ought to take care of this" means we have a choice but we also have an obligation. "We should take care of this" suggests we have more time and alternatives.

Example of the three:

Yes, you should rest your eyes. But if you want to appear fresh, you ought to use these eyedrops. In fact, if you want to avoid eye-trouble, you'd better use these eyedrops right now.

Another example—

You have a free ticket to Europe. You should consider using it now.

or—

You have a free ticket to Europe, and right now you have some free time. You ought to use it now.

or—

You have a free ticket to Europe; it expires next month. You'd better use it now.

This choice of words exemplifies the concept of power communication: apparently interchangeable terms often aren't perfect parallels.

Why and *What*

Why outpulls *What*—but *Why* has to be based on *What.*
A stiff-necked business-to-business insurance letter begins:

RE: Captive Professional Liability Insurance Survey
  (This is not a solicitation for insurance)
Dear Consultant:
A number of consultants' trade associations have expressed to us an interest in assessing the potential premium savings and/or improved coverage available by insuring through a CAPTIVE GROUP INSURANCE COMPANY, owned by the insureds themselves. (A brief explanation of such a captive

insurance arrangement is shown on the following page.)
In response, we propose to study the feasibility of such a program for you and your fellow consultants. The key questions to be addressed are . . .

Ask yourself: Wouldn't the letter be strengthened, made more readable, have more dynamite, and be better able to create a "This is aimed at *me*" reaction, if before drowning the message in a treacly "we" morass, the writer had thought, "I'd better tell them why"?

Emphasizing "What" betrays arrogance: The communicator assumes the very existence of his proposition is justification enough.

Wryly, perhaps, we can invoke *The John F. Kennedy Buyer Attitude Truism Rule.* The Rule is worth remembering when structuring a message to individuals you don't control:

- In this Age of Skepticism, the prospective buyer's first question isn't "What will it do?" but "What will it do for me?"

Our greed-driven society makes the Rule more significant that it would be if today's message-recipients were more homogenized and kindlier, as they were a couple of generations ago. To the John F. Kennedy Buyer Attitude Truism Rule we certainly should add *The Seller/Buyer Differential:*

- The seller's concern: What it is. The buyer's concern: What it will do for him.

The buyer doesn't want to buy "stuff." The buyer wants either a benefit or something for nothing. Catering to the buyer's selfish attitude is more logical than bypassing it. By emphasizing the buyer's concern instead of the seller's concern, true communicators bury and disguise their castor oil in a chocolate soda.

No "Buts" About It

After you've finished writing a piece of force-communication, use the "search" key to reexamine uses of the word *But.*

But is a condition changer, and that's why a power communicator can't throw it into the hopper with other automatic words such as *and.* We pay attention to longer words, but too often we unconsciously initiate a negative swivel by too-casual use of *but.*

One of the 30,000 or so limited edition "collectibles" tied to the 500th anniversary of the first voyage of Columbus had this paragraph:

> *It is trite to say that the brochure I've enclosed cannot*
> *do this historic ship justice as she appears in these*
> *glorious works of art. But it is true just the same.*

Shakespeare said, "When sorrows come, they come not as single spies but in battalions." Starting this sorrowful paragraph with the incredibly poor wording "It is trite to say . . ." takes the heat off *but* for a moment . . . but only for a moment.

(Reexamine each *but* in my own comments under this subhead. See how each one turns the mood downward?)

So "But it is true all the same" not only doesn't rescue the paragraph; it adds even more tears to the soup.

Use *But* to uplift, to bring forth a revelation, to spring an "Aha!" upon the reader, not to underscore a negative. (*But* can reverse a negative statement. See Chapter 6, "*But* as a Negative/ Positive.")

When to Replace *But* with *And*

Consider replacing *but* with *and* when you want to take the guilt out of consequence:

> *Of course we shouldn't consider doing this . . . but of course we're going to do it.*

or—

> *Of course we shouldn't consider doing this . . . and of course we're going to do it.*

But has so much negative power its misuse can shoot you in the foot. Understanding when to use the word and when to avoid it is significant ammunition . . . as the next section verifies.

Additional Uses of *But*

The previous sections point out how *but* is to grammar what hot pepper is to seasoning—a potent additive to be used sparingly and with exquisite care. But *but* has great versatility. (Note how the first *but* in the previous sentence generated a "Sure, I was expecting a *but* reaction.")

To add sarcasm to a negative, replace *isn't* with *anything but*: Instead of "Your message isn't subtle," use "Your message is anything but subtle." The reverse, for unprovable or attackable superlative-positives, is *Nothing but*: Instead of "We sell the freshest grapefruit," use "We sell nothing but fresh grapefruit."

Can and Its Confrères

Can suggests *conditional* ability. It differs from *May*, which also suggests ability but is even more conditional; and from *Will*, which is nonconditional.

This difference is why fund-raisers don't say, "*Can* you help us?" They say, "*Will* you help us?" The difference between suggesting ability and suggesting willingness is profound, when one recognizes the tonnage *guilt* adds to a sales argument.

Would you use *can* or *will* for this statement?

Apply one of those old-fashioned heat salves and everybody in the room [can/will] smell it for the whole day.

We want *will* because we want the deliberate effect, not the accidental effect.

Even though the word *can* is conditional, it adds power to half-claims.

Take a look at this headline, which appears to be an attempt to circumvent government regulatory agency objections:

WE MAKE NO CLAIMS AND WE MAKE NO PROMISES. ALL WE DO IS TELL YOU WHAT OTHERS SAY—AND ADD OUR OWN 100% MONEY-BACK GUARANTEE

Now look at the same headline with the word *can* inserted three times:

*WE CAN MAKE NO CLAIMS AND WE CAN
MAKE NO PROMISES. ALL WE CAN DO IS
TELL YOU WHAT OTHERS SAY—
AND ADD OUR OWN 100% MONEY-BACK
GUARANTEE*

The difference between *make* and *can make*, between *do* and
can do, is the difference between what appears to be casual arrogance and what appears to be straining against a leash. The latter
phrase says, subtly, "It's there, but *they* won't let us say it."

(For more on the difference between *can* and *may* see "'In
Loco Parentis' Can Mean a 'Plumb Loco' Parent," chapter 11.)

Warming Up an Imperative with "Will You"

Adding "Will you?" to a statement changes a cold imperative
to a warm request.

Instead of "Call me tomorrow with a progress report," for
warmth—which you may not want—write or say, "Call me tomorrow with a progress report, will you?"

The difference between the statement with and without "will
you?" suggests a use in good guy/bad guy mailings. The bad guy
writes a forceful letter, demanding action; the good guy writes an
additional enclosure, a conciliatory note using "will you?" as a
softened hook.

"Will you?" follows the classic benefit of *will* as opposed to
can: It puts the decision in the hands of the target . . . valuable
for fund-raising, rapport-enhancing, and employee morale-build-
ing.

Just: Increased Immediacy

The word *just* adds immediacy.

Your accountant might write, "I've checked the records and see that . . ."—which is why he or she is an accountant, not a power communicator.

We'd instantly add the words *our* and *you*— "I've checked our records and see that you . . ." because we're motivators, not reporters. But hold it! If we're motivating, isn't timeliness one of our weapons?

Adding the word *just* is like adding monosodium glutamate to a not-quite-spiced soup: "I've just checked our records and see that you . . ."

How about *only* as a synonym for *just*, not to show immediacy but to show singularity?

Just and *only* are usually interchangeable . . . but not always.

An example of an exception:

"What's different? Just the name."

or—

"What's different? Only the name."

A more venerable example: "Only you can prevent forest fires."

Only projects a more positive singularity than *just* when you want to show a deliberate selection. *Just* is more casual, possibly because of the other use of the word ("Just sign and mail the card").

Only can add specificity. As a synonym for *just*, this principle doesn't apply. But as a qualifier, *only* specifies the exclusion of all other circumstances. Without *only*, exclusion is inferred, not specified. Emphasizing *only* underscores the exclusion. Which of these shows the greatest degree of exclusion?

- Wetting the brush interferes with its top performance.
- This brush works best when the pad is dry.
- This brush works best only when the pad is dry.
- This brush works best *only* when the pad is dry.

Save: How to Follow Up to Validate the Word

"Save" is an imperative. Following it up with a description of the *result* of saving eliminates the dangerous suggestion that the reader, viewer, or listener has to *work* to get the result.

Example:
- [IMPERATIVE] "Save $20!"
- [RESULT] "That $20 stays in *your* pocket."

Much as writers love the word *you*, "You'll Save" isn't as vigorous as "Save."

Happen or *Occur*?

Happen is stronger than *occur*. If you want that extra .0001% of strength, write, "This couldn't happen," not, "This couldn't occur."

Is It *Right*? Or Is It *Correct*?

Which is correct? "That's right" or "That's correct"?

Either one, depending on whether you want convivial agreement or acolyte agreement. "That's correct" casts you in an arm's-length, professorial posture: You're giving a student a grade. "That's right" is an enthusiastic statement of harmony.

Does this mean we should always use "That's right"? No, no. It means we should evaluate the position we want to assume, relative to the other party.

Far and *Away*—Distant But Not Identical

The words *far* and *away* aren't interchangeable.

You're writing advertising for a real estate development. Which phrase works better?

- Far from the city's noise and grime . . .
- Away from the city's noise and grime . . .

You could opt for either, depending on the image you're trying to transmit. *Far*, the more specific of the two words, may be *too* far for those who like everything about urban life except noise and grime. We can extrapolate from this example *The Pinpoint Description Rule:*

- Within the sought target-group, specificity attracts; outside the target-group, specificity may repel.

To make this Rule valid, you'd better know who your targets are. Let's not repel possible buyers or donors.

Reply or *Respond*?

Reply is preferable to *Respond* when you want your target to feel he or she can inquire without obligation. *Respond* is preferable when you want your target to sense a minor commitment.

Respond is a more upscale word than *reply*, but patrician/ proletariat terminology isn't a factor in this context. Rather, we have a simple rhetorical conclusion: When you reply, you make no commitment; when you respond, you do.

A reply is just an answer. A response is an answer-*plus*. So when we write, "Please respond within 15 days," we can (however subliminally) terrify the reader.

The flip-side of this point is using the word when it applies to *you.* You don't just reply to a complaint or a question, you respond to it.

Is It *Free* . . . or Is It *Complimentary?*

Awareness of the difference between *complimentary* and *free* can result in a word-change which adds both impact and verisimilitude to your offer.

When appealing to status, use the word *complimentary*. No, it doesn't have the raw power *free* has; but it does have a connotation *free* never can match: *exclusivity*.

Consider *complimentary* as a replacement for *free* not only when you're communicating with upscale targets but, more to the point, when you're communicating with *would-be* upscale targets. The would-be's always are more sensitive to such treatment than their genuine counterparts.

We can formulate *The "Free" Effectiveness Rule:*

- The lower down the economic scale we go, the more effective the word *free* becomes.

Why? Three reasons underscore this conclusion:

1. Groups below the mid-range economic level respond more quickly and openly to an appeal to greed.
2. Groups below the mid-range economic level respond more quickly and openly to an appeal to envy, which is a combination of greed and guilt.
3. Advertisers make fewer "free" offers to groups below the mid-range economic level, so such offers have greater impact than they do on those accustomed to such incentives.

Don't misinterpret the "Free" Effectiveness Rule. This magic word works and works and works . . . on all levels. We're exploring intensity, not weakness.

A Big Little Word: *Discount*

The word *Discount* is becoming a magic trigger word with the potency *Free* and *New* used to have.

Who can resist a discount? For generations merchants have known many shoppers don't care what something costs; it's what it's been reduced from.

Within the limits of FTC acceptability, discounts not only are "in"; they work.

The analytical communicator admires the way a mail order insurance writer swamped the recipient with discounts in a recent piece. Headed, "Veterans: Important Notice," the subhead used the key word:

Rate Discounts are available that can help you save money on your auto insurance.

An outsider might snicker at the discounts and the weaseling, but the recipient isn't likely to. Here's the key copy:

> *. . . YOU ARE AMONG THOSE DRIVERS WHO MAY BE ELIGIBLE FOR SUBSTANTIAL RATE "DISCOUNTS" UNDER THIS AUTO INSURANCE PLAN.*
>
> *This coverage entitles drivers who qualify to the following rate discounts and SAVINGS:*
>
> *"SAFE DRIVER DISCOUNT"*
> *"RETIREMENT DISCOUNT"*
> *"DEFENSIVE DRIVING COURSE DISCOUNT"*
> *"MULTI-CAR DISCOUNT"*

We might ask the writer why he or she put those words inside quotation marks . . . and used "among" when other exclusivity-laden words exist; but the power point: This one little section used the magic word six times. (Proof of its magic: Repetition doesn't seem to dull it.)

More Little Words: *Many* and *Most*

Many and *Most* are weakeners as often as they're strengtheners.

Why? Because they're qualifiers, and qualifiers are weakeners. *Many people* is weaker than *People*. *Most people* is weaker than *People*.

What do we do when we can't make a flat, comprehensive claim? We write around the circumstance. But (here's that word

But again!) we'd never do what this catalog writer did, destroying his own sales argument with the word *Most* in the headline:

RID YOUR HOME OF MOST ROACHES,
MICE, RATS, FLEAS, ANTS
& OTHER HOUSEHOLD PESTS

Most roaches? The reader envisions a guest gagging politely during a formal dinner, then whispering to the hostess, "My dear, you seem to have roaches." The hostess sniffs, "Oh, we only have two of them."

The creative problem isn't unique. We have to write around the circumstance because apparently the gadget doesn't get rid of all the pests. So our headline might begin, "Bugs and Rats Running Wild? They'll Run The Other Way When You Plug This In!"

(Another one of the power communicator's pet peeves is here too: the ampersand. We see "&" and think of the names on a law office door.)

The Danger Implicit in *Read*

Add to your list of danger-words this apparently harmless candidate: *read*.

Why? *Read* is work. It requires education and time. So when your message is pitched below the highest levels, or when reading isn't part of what you're selling, weigh the possibility of adding apparent reader comfort by a simple switch. Instead of "Read what users say," write, "Look at what users say."

For that matter, look at what writers say, especially—if you're in a benevolent frame of mind—this one. (Actually, no one should fear asking anyone who deliberately bought this book . . . to read.)

One of the Littlest Words: *Oh*

Oh before a concession statement reduces the essence of the concession:

> *"Waterproof. A drop or two might sneak through. That's all."*

or—

> *"Waterproof. Oh, a drop or two might sneak through. That's all."*

Another of the Littlest Words: The Invaluable *So*

So has two remarkable properties:
1. It creates a transition where none exists.
2. It adds verisimilitude to a questionable claim.

An example of the first type of wonder the word *so* can impart:

> *This unusual work of collectible art on porcelain is the result of three separate firings, the last of which fuses the 24-karat gold ornamentation permanently into its rim and backstamp. So I urge you to mail or phone your reservation this very day.*

Without "so," the two sentences are unconnected. They need a third transitional sentence. With "so" the sentences still are unconnected, but they *apparently* are connected. *So* fools the eye and its accompanying comprehension.

An example of the second type of wonder the word *so* can impart:

This means we're able to offer you a wonderful rate, substantially below the rates so many others must pay.

Without "so" we have an unsubstantiated claim—"many others." The word *so* implicitly generates reader-acceptance.

Belongs Versus *Should Be*

To imply superiority or admiration, *belongs* is stronger than *should be*.

You may not even see a relationship between the two verbs until you look at them in a comparative context:

- This painting [belongs] [should be] in the Louvre.
- That jump [belongs] [should be] in the Guinness Book of Records.
- The statement, "To imply superiority or admiration, 'belongs' is stronger than 'should be,'" [belongs] [should be] in *Bartlett's Quotations*.

Belongs gives us an extra ounce of enthusiasm when we're approving or selling. *Should be* lets us back off a little without abandoning our endorsement.

Learn and *Earn*

Learn and *earn* suggest work. In unsolicited offers, replace these words with others which have a less-strenuous overtone.

Notice, please—this proposition limits itself to unsolicited offers. Actually, it rates only about 50% on "This is the information you asked for" mailings too.

"You'll discover how to" is a bright replacement for "You'll learn how to" and "You'll carry $75,000 a year to the bank" paints a less arduous word-image than "You'll earn $75,000 a year." (This is in the *promotional* pre-benefit phase. Learning and earning are *results*, which suggests usefulness in post-sale literature.)

Why exclude half the instances in which you're communicating with somebody who asked for information? Because about half the time the nature of what you're selling needs *learn* or *earn* to validate your original claim that brought in the inquiry.

Bring and *Offer*

As a verb, *bring* can generate greater acceptance than *offer* because *bring* assumes a relationship.

Parallel examples:
- I think you'll be as proud to own this Collection as we are to offer it to you.
- I think you'll be as proud to own this Collection as we are to bring it to you.

Bring suggests mutual acceptance; *offer* suggests the possibility of rejection. In communications to those other than existing customers or clients, consider using *offer* once, then switching to *bring*.

Spend, Pay, and *Owe*

The power communicator uses words such as *spend, pay,* and

owe with the caution they deserve. These words have negative connotations even when the reference isn't financial.

In conversation we might say, "I spent a night at that hotel," but in print somehow it looks threatening:

> *When you spend a night with us, you'll finally know what luxury means.*

The suggested replacement:

> *When you stay with us for even one night, you'll finally know what luxury means.*

Similarly we can blunt the reader's budding enthusiasm with this type of language:

> *I want you to pay careful attention to what I'm about to tell you.*

No dollars are involved, but we're paying. Does that establish a subliminally uncomfortable position for us? Aside from the imperious tone of this sentence, any reader—writer or not—can think of a less-parental way of putting this same thought.

Too and *Also*

Too and *also* are another pair of words whose connotations are similar but not identical.

The communicator can profit from recognizing the tiny difference: *Too* is more personal, a closer tie than *also*, which has an arm's-length overtone.

If you're communicating with somebody who doesn't know

you, assumption of a relationship can be a turnoff. Verisimilitude may call for starting with more reserved terminology, then imperceptibly adding familiarity to the rhetoric.

So initial seasoning is light, using words such as *also* ("You also know . . ." instead of "You know, too . . ."), which hold back familiarity. As the communication builds pace, changing *also* to *too* is imperceptible but effective.

Arm's-length terms usually are less effective emotionally than familiar terms. You may *want* to transmit the impression of arm's length, but be aware of the difference between *prior to*—a mild pomposity—and *before*, a normal conversational term.

Speaking of mild pomposities, power communicators never use *purchase* as a verb. And they can be drummed out of the corps for using *for*, a nineteenth-century term, instead of *because*.

Really and *Frankly*

Really is a better power word than *Frankly*.

A curmudgeonish opinion: *Frankly* could disappear without mourning. To those who want ammunition before firing, here are three reasons for punching the search key and replacing *Frankly* with *Really*—or dropping the adverb altogether:

1. *Really* is less judgmental.
2. *Really* is more convivial.
3. *Really* is less soap-box "I'm above you."

Stories, Histories, Legends, and Lore

If you're a story-teller, what do you tell? Stories? Histories? Legends? Lore?

The words *aren't* parallel. Mother tells a story to her daughter. The professor recites a history. The spellbinder recounts a legend. Lore doesn't enter into the mix because it isn't parallel.

So *legend* has an aura of exotic entertainment the other words lack. That makes it the proper word only if circumstances permit specificity. *Story* is the safe generalization.

Lean . . . with a Little Marbling

Good writing is lean, but insert auxiliary words when you'd foster confusion by leaving them out.

An example of too-lean writing is this sentence from an energy-conservation letter:

> *By participating in the Conservation Incentive*
> *Program, you'll help lower energy demand during peak*
> *periods.*

Maybe it's clear to you the first time you read it; maybe not. See the problem? The word *lower* is a verb *and* an adjective. You plow ahead with an assumption, which might or might not be accurate. Adding one auxiliary word makes misinterpretation impossible:

> *By participating in the Conservation Incentive*
> *Program, you'll help to lower energy demand during*
> *peak periods.*

If the verb had been *move* the auxiliary word wouldn't have been necessary. Decide to use or leave out auxiliaries on a case-by-case basis.

Various: Search and Destroy

A suggestion regarding a single word—*various*. Here's a word which quietly weakens many communications. Hit your search key and destroy *various* when you see it in constructions such as

- You'll be able to pinpoint various market segments.
- This compact disc has various compositions by Haydn.
- Various executives misuse the word *various*.

In: Search and *Maybe* Destroy

The word *in* after a superlative adds weaseling pomposity for no reason at all. Examples: "The best in mailing lists"; "the finest in furniture." The value of *in*? Zero.

Tests, Quizzes, and Ballots

A peculiar mailing by a leading publisher of list data has a lift letter inviting me to "Take this test, to see if you've made the correct decision."

Is this supposed to excite? A *test* puts the mailer in a superior position, which readers resent; a *quiz* would have taken the brutal edge off the implication there's a qualification they might not meet; "What's YOUR opinion?" transmits a genuine desire to know what the reader thinks; a *ballot* makes *the reader* superior, the most acceptable relationship of all.

A Handful of Wordlets

- To vs. *into*: Forget your grammar book for this one. "Bring your Discount Coupon to Our Store" seems less work and suggests less of a commitment than "Bring your Discount Coupon into our store."
- *Every day* is stronger than *daily*: "We compound your interest every day."
- Use *skill* for art, *expertise* for services such as insurance and finance, *craftsmanship* for construction. For occasional extra power—but never more than once in a single communication—swap words.
- The difference between *always* and *constantly*: Compare your own reactions to these two sentences— "We're always adding new discounts for you"; "We're constantly adding new discounts for you." *Constantly* is softer but more dynamic because it suggests ongoing *individual* actions rather than an ongoing *single* action.

Thesaurus: Power Communication Brontosaurus?

As often as not, unlimbering Roget's isn't the answer. Would a thesaurus have helped the writer who referred to his company as "among the most respected publishers" instead of the equally simple-to-write "one of the most respected publishers." The difference is fractional; but *among* makes the company one of the mob while *one of* suggests singularity. Why bother with neutral (ergo, denigrating) words?

Would a thesaurus have helped this hara-kiri line glaring at us from the moment of truth, the order form of a consumer offer?

*YES, please send me, right away, the referenced items
I've selected.*

Referenced items? Great heavens, couldn't the writer suppress
his intellectual snobbery for ten more minutes—until the order
form was safely processed?

Would a thesaurus have been of any value to the writer
whose thin sense of reader excitement generated this deadly line
of copy about art objects?

*The manufacturer has told us the quantity we are to
receive will be small.*

Look at the mess here: *Manufacturer* (instead of, say, *producer*)
for art? *Quantity* (instead of *allocation*) to suggest a limited number?
"We are to receive" (instead of using *our* before *allocation*) as a
bumbling comprehension-delayer?

A thesaurus would have been helpful to the writer of the
next example—but only as valuable as the writer's decision to
suppress vocabulary and switch over to words paralleling what the
reader accepts as a positive goad. The writer's competence isn't
in question; it's the dedication to reader excitement that flagged
here.

SUBSCRIBE TODAY!
Here's what your peers have said about
The Office Professional.

What is it about that word *peer* that makes us think we're
either being judged by a jury or becoming part of a pre-teen focus
group?

Overstretching for Colorful Words

Overstretching for colorful words can damage reader empathy. Stay within acceptable bounds.

Once again we see hard evidence that strong direct response writing can require the discipline of vocabulary *suppression*. Fund raisers have to be especially careful; when their message reflects a fanatical devotion to their cause, it's time for disinterested third-person proofreading.

An example is a money-plea. A journeyman communicator might have written:

Our medical wizards worked all through the night . . .

The copy, as it actually appeared in the mailed appeal, splashed too much color on a key word:

Our medical wizards slaved all through the night . . .

"Slaved" smacks of involuntary servitude, not a happy way to raise money. Professional wording would have been:

Our medical wizards battled all through the night . . .

The point of this proposition isn't word-juggling. Rather, it's the suggestion that if you can't think of an *apt* spectacular word, don't accept an inapt spectacular word. "Worked" is superior to "slaved" because "worked" doesn't call attention to itself *as a word* without furthering the sales argument.

Upgraded Terminology

Upgrade terminology when a different word can enhance the "Only you . . ." impression.

A Rolls-Royce isn't a car; it's a motorcar. It doesn't have a motor; it has an engine. It isn't upholstered in leather; it's upholstered in Connolly hydes (their spelling, not mine).

A movie doesn't have an opening; it has a premiere. The premiere isn't just a movie; it's a motion picture. It doesn't have a musical background; it has a musical score. The secondary actors aren't day-players; they're listed under "Also Starring . . ." The backer isn't the money-man; he's the executive producer.

These euphemisms don't cost a quarter. They're free. They not only make the individual feel good, they add import to the product itself. The buyer feels he or she is getting a little more. Everybody wins when *carton* becomes *presentation box*.

Look for the opportunities. You don't need an eagle eye to spot envelope copy such as

ATTENTION: Your free *membership decal is enclosed!*

Yes, changing "decal" to "emblem" involves typesetting one more character. But we've taken the message out of its bumper-sticker connotation.

Upgrading can be especially valuable when describing quantities. For example, "Quantity is limited," transformed to "Our allocation is limited," adds urgency and exclusivity to a mundane phrase.

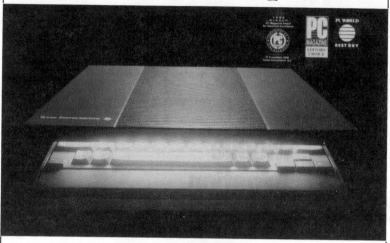

Fig. 3.6

This manufacturer states (quite properly) that its notebook computer is 1.4" <u>thin</u> and 4.4 lbs. <u>light</u>. Had the writer said the computer is "just 1.4" thick and weighs only 4.4 lbs.," the reader would not have reacted to thinness and lightness but would have thought "thick" and "weight."

Mobster gets new trial

NEW YORK — An appellate court panel
on Friday ordered a new trial for Anthony
"Fat Tony" Salerno, the reputed former
head of the Genovese crime family, and seven
associates.

Three judges of the 2nd U.S. Circuit Court
of Appeals reversed the racketeering
convictions and said the case was tainted by
the exclusion of testimony that might have
helped the defendants.

Fig. 3.7
*The news story itself refers to the individual as
the reputed former head of the Genovese crime
family, but the word Mobster in the headline
has preconditioned the reader to disregard
reputed. Harsh key words set the reader's
attitude in cement.*

As Much As or Up to?

Let's add some *wham* to a journeyman line—

Save up to $81!

Nothing wrong, you say? You're right. It isn't *wrong*; it just
isn't as exciting as it might be. Tinker with it for five seconds and
you have—

Save as much as $81!

What's the difference? This: The hairline edge for excitement
goes to "as much as," over "up to." Nitpicking does pay off in a

business which measures effectiveness the right way—by fractions of a percent of response.

Thick Is Always Thick

"Thick" seems *thick,* even when you use the word to suggest thinness. So using *thick* when you don't want something to be regarded as thick is a confusing message. Instead of "It's just ¾″ thick," write either "It's just ¾″ thin"—which may be confusing— or "It's just ¾″ in height." Why not "It's just ¾″ tall?" Because *tall* has the same singularity of interpretation as *thick.*

Older folks like to say, "I'm just 86 years young." The double-take is deliberate; but they aren't power communicators. This use does point out the right time to misuse words which generate instant image: *satire.*

Application or *Invitation?*

Don't change the implied relationship from element to element of a sales argument.

Writers tend to run on tracks, and if we're not on the lookout for violations of this point, we use standard terminology. Terminology might be correct, but the "right" word may be inconsistent with Power Communication.

Application, a common word we use for response devices, exemplifies this point. If you tell a target individual, "You're one of a select few," maintain this tone. You've issued an invitation, and the person who invites should stay in character.

Accompanying this message with a form labeled "Application" takes off the silk glove and slaps the face. *Invitation* says to

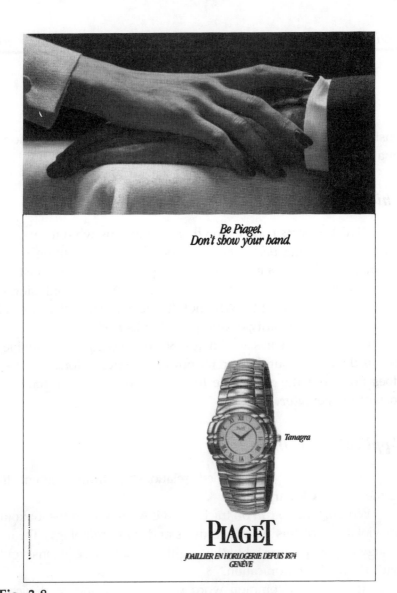

Fig. 3.8

This message, highly flawed because the message seems to be incoherent, nonetheless follows the principle of starting with a positive, then using a negative for emphasis. "Be . . ." precedes "Don't . . .," but the meaning of this advertisement stays locked within the writer's own comprehension.

your target: You're slightly super-equal. *Application* says to your target: You're slightly sub-equal. Where *Invitation* can't apply, *Confidential Reply Form* maintains the one-on-one relationship.

When Is *Notice* Stronger than *Offer?*

The beginner leaps blindly into the fray, saying, "*Offer* is positive and *notice* is neutral, so *offer* is the better word."

Is it? Maybe. Maybe not. The author of this book made the change *from* "offer" *to* "notice" on a piece of copy for a public utility which didn't want to suggest it was "pitching" the reader. *Notice* not only has greater verisimilitude; it becomes a more positive word than offer because we give the reader the impression he or she is forming a positive response instead of reacting to our trying to sell something.

No writer can remember every procedure and every exception. The key to this chapter is the mild admonition: Choose words as though your job depends on it. It might.

Chapter 4
The Definite Versus the Indefinite

The word *a* is not only the shortest article, it's the weakest. Dynamic communication usually replaces the word in constructions whose reader interpretation influences the decision to respond.

Let's not overcomplicate this. Go over anything you've written and circle every use of the word *a* or *an—an* issue, *a* week, *an* opportunity, *a* decision.

You won't be able to make logical replacements for all the uses, nor do you really want to. What you're looking for is unnecessary *weakness* stemming from the indefinite article. *The* is the definite equivalent. Will replacing an occasional *a* with *the* strengthen the message by .0001%? Then do it.

Each, every, and *all* are considerably higher than *the* or *one* on the definite-scale. The three words are parallel, but their degree of power differs, as this chapter explains.

Usually, specifics have greater power than generalities. The professional communicator recognizes a *mutual* value: Some descriptions actually gain strength from avoiding specificity.

(For an exception to this principle, look at the section in this chapter entitled, "Specifics Are Stronger than Generalities . . . Except . . .")

Are these differences subtle . . . and if so, are they of any value, recognizing the weakness of subtlety itself in power communication? To the communicator dedicated to maximized power,optimizing the mixture of specifics and generalities, defi-

nites and indefinites, is an indispensable screwdriver in the rhetorical tool-bag.

The to Suggest Exclusivity

Insert or remove the word *the* to suggest exclusivity or availability.

If you've read chapter 1, you already know the difference
between these two approaches:

> *George T. Murdoch, associate editor of Science*
> *Monthly, writes . . .*

or—

> *George T. Murdoch, the associate editor of Science*
> *Monthly, writes . . .*

Right: The word *the* adds stature to George T. Murdoch by
suggesting he's the *only* associate editor. Without the definite article, George T. Murdoch may be one of many.

"He is one of few musicians who can perform the Paganini
Concerto" isn't as selective as "He is one of the few musicians
who can perform the Paganini Concerto."

The difference between these two versions of the same information is quickly obvious:

- *Version 1:* The plates, depicting scenes of the Civil
  War era, provided funds for construction of a new
  museum building.
- *Version 2:* The plates, depicting scenes of the Civil
  War era, provided the funds for construction of a
  new museum building.

The difference between "providing funds" and "providing *the* funds" is the difference between one of many and singularity. The difference between definite and indefinite can be useful in both directions.

The has serendipity built into it, because switching to the definite article sometimes forces the writer to restructure the rest of the sentence, injecting specifics to make *the* logical. Occasionally you'll be able to replace *a* with a word considerably more definite than *the,* such as "one month" instead of "a month."

When to Use *One* Instead of *A*

Use *one* instead of *a* when you're establishing superiority.

A needn't be banished to Niflheim; the power communicator simply recognizes the possibility of substitution.

Which of these is more likely to have the reader saying, "Wow!"?

The gem in each earring is a full carat . . .

or—

The gem in each earring is one full carat . . .

Another preference of *one* over *a*: to add *stature* to a number. "More than one million sold" is more impressive than "More than a million sold." "Your private discount is one hundred dollars" shows *you're* more impressed with the discount you're offering than you would be had you said, "Your private discount is a hundred dollars." "He's one hundred years old" shows more awe than "He's a hundred years old."

The foundation for the superiority of *one* over *a* is the generic superiority of the definite over the indefinite. So the reverse works when you *want* a throwaway: "Heck, it was only a hundred dollars" looks down on the amount; "Heck, it was only one hundred dollars" fails as a throwaway—because of **The Formality Rule:**

- All *formal statements fail as throwaways.*

WARNING: Overused, *one* is (sequentially) pompous, uninventive, and annoying. That's why "How would you like to have a million dollars?" may create a more receptive attitude than "How would you like to have one million dollars?"

Changing *A* or *The* to *Your*

Changing *a* or *the* to *your* suggests immediate possession-recognition.

Conventional advertising generates a line such as:

Here's the *different* kind of tobacco satisfaction.

Emphasis is on the *what*, not the *who*, typical of conventional advertising. The typical direct response version adapts its classic one-on-one approach, making one word change:

Here's your *different* kind of tobacco satisfaction.

The whole meaning of the statement changes if the writer leans hard on the article or the word "you":

- Here's *the* different kind of tobacco satisfaction.
- Here's *your* different kind of tobacco satisfaction.

Changing both word *and* emphasis can change the message.

Sometimes casual insertion of the word *you* adds more strength than beating it about the head and shoulders by underlining or italics. Be careful of overselling by overemphasizing target-possession.

Generic = Indefinite

Generic adjectives can't compete with amplifying adjectives.

This is one of the separators that leaves beginners, pretenders, and dilettantes in one pile and master wordsmiths in another stack, far smaller.

The children of a lesser god use words like *special* and *great* and *wonderful* as their crutches. These are generics, adding only confetti to the sales argument.

A mail order vitamin company says in its copy:

We've added an extra 500 mg of vitamin C to this special tablet.

Replacing the generic with an amplifier, copy would have read:

We've added an extra 500 mg of vitamin C to this enhanced tablet.

The difference may be fractional; fractions separate the two groups of writers.

Generic motivators run a slow second to genuine motivators, but they're immeasurably superior to negative motivators. Visualize a sales argument which begins, "You may never need what we want to sell you."

Would you give this opening an "A" in salesmanship?

No. Not in a piece of mail, part of the daily accumulation. Not in a space ad, competing for reader reaction with other space ads. Not in a television or radio commercial, whose first few words dictate gained or lost interest. We understand the motivation behind such an opening, but we don't understand the *choice* of this approach when so many other openings, which might grab and shake me, are lurking right there in the same keyboard.

So logical communication questions this fund-raising letter:

Dear Mr. Lewis,
You may never need us . . . but right now we need
you!
Of course, none of us likes to think about cancer. But
the sad fact is . . .

Why suggest the reader won't need you? Today's fund raising climate is murderously competitive, and a communication which plays hard melodies on the four primary motivational strings fear, exclusivity, guilt, and greed—still has a hard time of it.

Four paragraphs down, we have this one-line paragraph:

I'm writing to ask for your help.

Lacking other motivators, I'd have started with this, because it's a generic *guilt* plea. In my opinion, even though it isn't a specific and is ten years out of date, it's superior to the dangerous negative the writer used.

Each, All, and Every

You won't be misunderstood if you use *each* and *all* interchangeably. But you might not get the impact you intend.

(A quick parenthetical note: What's the difference between "You won't be misunderstood" and "You'll be understood"? The negative/positive differential is discussed in chapter 6.)

All suggests bulk and *each* suggests singularity. With this interpretation the differences become more apparent.

What circumstances would suggest using *each* or *all* for this communication?

> *The editor, the art director, the production manager,*
> *and the pressroom supervisor [each checks] [all check]*
> *the blueline.*

If we want to imply individual personal and thorough attention, we use *each*; if we want to imply a greater number of people, we use *all*.

You can apply the principle to statements such as . . .

- [Each person] [All the people] on our staff [has/ have] been granted top secret clearance.
- [Each of] [All] our monitor screens exceed[s] government requirements for radiation suppression.
- [Each diamond] [All the diamonds] in this group [has/have been] rated flawless by a certified gemologist.

When we want to split the difference between "each" and "all," the word "every" is at hand:

Every diamond in this group has been rated flawless by a certified gemologist.

Apparent Specificity: Mutating *Some* and *Many*

To enhance background information, look for the words *some* or *many* and replace them with ostensible authentication. *The Automatic Authentication Technique*:

■ Authenticate by adding the mantle of apparent importance.

Instead of, "We asked some customers," write, "We asked a representative sampling of our customers." Instead of, "The remedy many doctors prefer," write, "The remedy chosen by many doctors in a nationwide survey."

Note that we haven't removed "many"; we've enhanced it by authentication. Never let puffery extend to falsehood.

Note, too, the wording is, "Never let puffery extend to falsehood," not, "Puffery never should extend to falsehood," a considerably weaker imperative.

Specifics Are Stronger than Generalities . . . Except . . .

Usually specifics have greater impact than generalities. One exception is when the specific has less stature than the generality. A generic reference, avoiding specificity *which might lessen stature*, can add prominence.

An example: Typically, an individual might say, "I'm Mary Alice Barton, and I run the 'Cooking with Gas' Show on Station WXX-TV." It's specific, and it's accurate. But . . .

Specificity, stipulating the local nature of this celebrity, has less impact than a generality which lets the message recipient's own experiential background interpret the remark—to the presenter's benefit: "I'm Mary Alice Barton, and I run television's 'Cooking with Gas' Show."

The decision to use a specific or a generalization can't depend on blind adoration of specificity. Logic underlies every facet of power communication.

Chapter 5
Reducing Plurals to Singulars . . .
and Future to Present Tense

In any reference to message-recipients, singular is stronger than plural. The reader, viewer, or listener wants to think he or she is special. So when we start a television commercial with "Hey, all you folks who . . ." or a letter with, "I know many of you will . . ." we not only defoliate the delicate buds of rapport by our unwitting arrogance, but, worse, we say to somebody's fragile individuality: "You're one of a mob."

The poet Coleridge once referred to his craft as creating "the willing suspension of disbelief." Come on, fellow poets, let's give Coleridge his due. He obviously would have been successful as a power communicator.

Sure, those people out there know you mailed more than one letter. They know the newspaper or magazine printed more than one copy. They know the broadcast message coming through their set hasn't been transmitted on a private wave-length.

But in a zip-coded, area-coded, serial-numbered world they want to feel special. They want to feel chosen. And, oh, how easy it is for us to give them the pablum they crave.

Our arena isn't a vast seminar, where the guy with the microphone can't even see the bodies in the back row. We sell best when we're one-on-one.

A disclaimer:

Nobody (except those with the least buying power) wants to be the first to experiment with a product or service others might regard as goofy, oddball, or strange. If you're introducing a novelty, tying newness to an established base eliminates the discomfort of a "You're the only one" suggestion.

You . . . and How Many Others?

Here's a standard letter opening, mis-aimed at too big a target:

I'm delighted to be able to send this private notice to a relative handful of worthy persons.

Narrowed to zero in on the bull's-eye, the line reads:

I'm delighted you're among the relative handful of worthy persons to whom I'm able to send this private notice.

We could have written:

I'm delighted to be able to send you this private offer.

Is this more or less exclusive? Careful, now. In this instance we haven't optimized the pitch, because some readers will be uncomfortable *being the only apparent target.* Tying newness to an established base (in this case, an exclusive *group*) eliminates discomfort.

So the word *among* should send up the usual red flags. The difference between "You're *among* the very first . . ." and "You're *one of* the very first . . ." is a valuable fragment of the difference between singular and plural.

The Rule of Singulars, Plus You, Me, and Us

Generally, we're safe fastening our message to *The Rule of Singulars* and the ***Bulk Non-Exclusivity Rule***. The first Rule:

- When claiming exclusivity, stay in sync by using singular instead of plural.

The second Rule:

- Bulk excludes exclusivity.

These are easy to understand and easy to implement. After telling the reader, "Only you," don't let pressure seep out of your word-boiler by adding, ". . . plus those other guys." "Thousands of top suppliers of electronic components" is self-defeating.

We've all reacted negatively to the overbearing "You're going to love this . . ." assumption. Be sure your "You" message is congruent with ***The Rule of You, Me, and Us:***

- The sales wallop of *You* as recognizable target is fractional compared to *You* as decision-maker. The vendor should hold back the implication that he takes the reader's reaction for granted until his sales argument reaches the point of "Watch it, you could miss out."

This line from a brochure is intended to describe how a limited edition work of art comes to life:

. . . Then, wearing lint-free gloves, these craftspeople fit the fresh-minted golden coins into their sterling silver frames.

Reader interest declines in ratio to intrusion of others into the magic, private realm. So we pump pressure back into the copy by changing it to:

> *. . . Then, wearing lint-free gloves, these craftspeople fit each fresh-minted golden coin into its sterling silver frame.*

Still not satisfied? We could personalize the act—

> *. . . Then, wearing lint-free gloves, these craftspeople fit your fresh-minted golden coin into its sterling silver frame.*

Caution: As logical as the word *you* seems to be here, it isn't a knee-jerk inclusion. *You* loses potency when the reader reacts, "They're taking me for granted."

The amateur goes blundering through a sales pitch, regurgitating the word *you* whenever possible because all the books and articles say it's even more powerful than *free* or *new*. And so it is, used as a rapier and not as a bludgeon.

Loading up copy with surplus "you" references isn't a ready gateway to the Kingdom of Heaven. This is a subtle point the communicator has to sense . . . which is why "professional" communication can justify itself as a profession.

The Value of Group References: Downplaying Responsibility

When might you use a group reference instead of aiming at a single individual? The answer is *The Rule of Individual Pinpointing or Group Avoidance:*

Dear Friend,

You've worked far too hard to get where you are
to let medical expenses steal it away from you.

You've seen the statistics...costs for hospital care
have increased dramatically, just since the beginning
of the 1980s.

So, if you are relying on hospital insurance you
obtained even just a few years ago, you may be in
for a shock when you have a claim.

Deductibles, coinsurance and maximum benefits which
may have seemed reasonable before, now could leave you
stuck with hospital bills, after your current coverage
is "tapped out."

That's why you owe it to yourself to check out the
$2,000,000.00 group hospital insurance plan endorsed
by the National Association for the Self-Employed.

Its "100% coverage" could save your bank account from
expenses other plans could leave behind for you to pay.

Please send your enclosed Request for Information
card...the information is free and you're under no
obligation to buy or join anything.

Sincerely,

Judy D. Laube

Judy D. Laube
Director of Member Services

Fig. 5.1
*Count the number of times the writer uses you and your in this
little enclosure (found in the "If You're Self-Employed" envelope
shown in chapter 3).*

- Use a group reference when you want to downplay responsibility or depersonalize; use individual references when you want to emphasize responsibility or personalize.

Like many statements that seem abstruse when projected in limbo, this one comes clear when tied to examples. Consider the difference between these two statements:

- My parents told me . . .
- My mother and father told me . . .

The information is the same. The connotation differs. "My parents told me" is relatively indefinite. By not pinpointing a "who," the statement prevents an attack. The target is too muddy and nonspecific for the attacker to zero in; a parallel is the "chaff" a warplane drops to confuse radar-driven missiles . . . or the line, "They say that falling in love is wonderful." Who are "they"? Give us some names, please.

This point has value in establishing consensus. If a committee votes six to four to discard a proposal, you can flex your report to reflect the position you favor. Look at just a few of the many possibilities in presenting the same information:

- The committee rejected the proposal, six to four.
- Four of the ten directors voted in favor of the proposal.
- George, Harry, Bill, and Jim voted in favor of the proposal, but it lost.
- In a close vote, George, Harry, Bill, and Jim favored the proposal; six others voted against it.

Note, please, a useful principle of force-communication: The greater the need for justification, the greater the amount of explanation.

A secondary value of The Rule of Individual Pinpointing and Group Avoidance is *evading* explanation when you don't want the reader or listener to think you're trying to justify a position, conclusion, or reaction.

Implicit Tie or Implicit Separator

"They" or "them both" is a closer tie than "the two of them." This is because "the two of them" is an implicit separator. The phrase suggests no tie.

"Your presentation will hit them both" implies a common, simultaneous reaction. "Your presentation will hit the two of them" suggests individual and possibly disparate reactions.

"They both reacted strongly" indicates a single reaction by two persons. "The two of them reacted strongly" indicates two reactions which may or may not be identical. Leaving the determination of whether or not the reactions were identical to the message recipient abandons the communicator's role as power persuader.

The Relationship Between Seller and Sellee

"Us" combines more tightly than "You or [I/me]" or "You and [I/me]."

"Both of us" and "Neither one of us" are more comradely than "You and I" and "Neither you nor I," because the "Us" phrase is *in*clusive; separating you and me, even while linking us with "and," is *ex*clusive.

The benefit: The message sender subtly controls the relationship, including drawing the parties closer together by *sequential* use of "You/I" followed by "Us." A possible technique:

> *"Neither you nor I would be interested in nondescript art. Neither of us would acquire art which has almost no chance of value-appreciation. But you and I—both of us—would act quickly if we had the opportunity to acquire works by an established artist at an incredibly low price.*

The Law of Tenses, Applied

Don't assume that present-plus-future is always a higher road than present-plus-present. One of the challenges of direct response writing is having to make choices; add this Proposition to the list. *First* you decide what reaction you want to generate; *then* you decide which words (do) (will do) the generating.

Future Tense Is Tomorrow; Present Tense Is Now.

The value of this truism in force-communication is recognition of its flat obviousness. From it, we extrapolate *The Law of Tenses:*

- Present tense outsells future tense because the present is now, and your reader wants benefits now.

Why Present Tense Is the Most Relevant

Aside from timeliness, present tense is both more relevant and more involving than either future tense or past tense.

If you thought Beethoven's Ninth was good, you should try Turnberry's.

Behind you the cliff drops fifty feet to the Atlantic. To the front and left, the shore awaits any hooked shot.

On the fairway a cairn shows the way to the green, 455 yards distant. Par is four.

This could only be the ninth hole of the Ailsa course at Turnberry, one of the great golf courses, host to the 1977 and 1986 British Opens. Complementing it is a second championship course, the Arran, all within the 360-acre grounds.

The pleasures of Turnberry are not limited to golf. You can work-out in the hotel's pool, sauna and gym. Play billiards and tennis. Browse in the shops. Savour five-star cuisine. Or simply unwind in the Edwardian elegance of the lounges, gazing out on ocean and islands.

All this classical relaxation is easy to reach, as your Travel Agent – and our Reservations Desk – will confirm.

TURNBERRY HOTEL AND GOLF COURSES, SCOTLAND
Turnberry, Ayrshire, KA26 9LT, Scotland. For reservations telephone Toll Free:
BTH Inc (800) 211 1074   Orient Express (800) 237 1236   Leading Hotels (800) 223 6800

A member of *The Leading Hotels of the World*

Fig. 5.2
Here is an interesting use of tenses. Would the advertisement be more powerful if "thought" became "think" ("If you think Beethoven's Ninth is good, you should try Turnberry's")? Yes, because present tense is <u>now</u>, and the word "should" couples better with present than with past.

This doesn't eliminate the value of past and future tenses; rather, it *classifies* them:

Use past tense to establish a historical base; use present tense to establish position.

The tense classification concept isn't a truism, because in this context position refers to placement in perception, not placement in time.

Example:

I wrote these words.

Use of past tense places the writer's action in the past.

I am the author of these words.

Use of present tense eliminates time as an element of perception; immediacy enhances the positions of both writer and words.

The Value of Immediacy for Broadcast Copy

Immediacy is a selling partner even more valuable for radio and television copy.

"Here is . . ."; "Here now . . ."; "Look for . . ."; the future/present hybrid "You'll find . . ."—all match the immediacy of the medium itself.

Availability is more noticeable in broadcast copy. The impact of a verbal "Right now" is more emphatic than the same words in print media.

"Sale ends tomorrow!" has greater impact in an evening radio or television spot than in a newspaper whose timing has to be loosely tied to the day, not the hour. "24 hours from now" is an explicit interval, impossible for print media to match.

A Powerful Exception

Simple enough. Now, let's refine the generality to take advantage of a powerful exception:

Tying future to present tells the reader: "This will be for all eternity."

Compare the meanings of these two approaches:

This is the seventh notification we've sent you. It's the last one.

or—

This is the seventh notification we've sent you. It will be the last one.

The message is the same. The first wording is a statement of position. The second is the voice of doom. Tying the present to the future tells the recipient: Throughout the annals of recorded time, you never will hear from us again. Use this tie not only for threats but for promises such as guarantees.

Has Become or *Is?*

Has become instead of *is* transforms an event from current fact into evolutionary news. Compare these two sentences:

SINCE 1735 THERE HAS NEVER BEEN A QUARTZ BLANCPAIN WATCH.
AND THERE NEVER WILL BE.

The ultra-slim watch

Expressing the essential. The first masterpiece in the art of watchmaking is portrayed by ideal perfection in the mechanical watch. The discreetness of the dial and the simplicity of its lines give this work of art a remarkable balance and a refined elegance.

The slimness of this movement, less than 1.75 mm in height, demands faultless workmanship and requires all the talent and skills of the master watchmaker who assembles and polishes it. In gold or platinum, several hundred ultra-slim watches, individually controlled, numbered and signed, leave Blancpain's workshops each year.

BLANCPAIN

Information from BLANCPAIN SA – CH-1348 Le Brassus – Switzerland – Tel. 21-845 40 92 – Fax 21-845 41 88

Fig. 5.3

Tying the future tense to the present—or in this example, both present and past—validates claims for the future, transforming those claims from dreams or speculation into commitment. The psychological effect is considerably stronger.

> *Managed care is the fastest-growing trend in healthcare.*

or—

> *Managed care has become the fastest-growing trend in healthcare.*

You can see the benefits both ways. Eliminating evolutionary overtones with *is* not only emphasizes the "now" aspect but also typifies the kind of flat, unequivocal statement so many arguments demand. Emphasizing evolutionary overtones with *has become* not only underscores superiority but also typifies the timeliness so many arguments demand.

Exceptions abound; but mistakes of aim and timing are rare when the communicator aims at a single target and does it now.

Chapter 6
Can Negatives Be Positive?

"**D**on't start a selling argument with don't."

Any communicator learns the dogma: Positives outsell negatives. And how right that is . . . usually.

We don't have to be professional psychologists (although it helps!) to realize why: We *usually* want our target readers to perform a positive act as the result of our exhortation. Admonitions starting with *No* or *Not* or *Can't* or *Don't*—even "Don't delay"—suggest inaction rather than action.

But when we break through the chains of our own preconceived prejudices, we certainly have to admit: Negatives have value. We *usually* use positives to open a sales argument, then use negatives for spice and emphasis. So we formulate *The Negative Validation Rule:*

■ Negatives validate the positives.

The Positive Superiority Principle

Positives are superior to negatives *as motivators* in about 80 percent of power communication messages. So, remembering that qualifier—*as motivators*—we can have 80 percent faith in *The Positive Superiority Principle:*

■ Positives usually outpull negatives. So don't start your selling argument with "Don't."

That's exactly the way the Rule states itself. Normal easy usage prefers to state it this way:

Don't start your selling argument with "Don't"
because negatives don't pull as well as positives.

Do you see the difference? The message is identical. But by starting with the negative—"Don't"—the Rule would suggest you're at fault for something. Negatives feed antagonisms; positives soothe antagonisms.

Don't has another weight hanging on its back: It says, "Stop."

Now, the Hedge

Don't has positive uses. So don't abandon *don't* forever. The Rule just suggests you avoid *opening* with it. We all have seen hundreds, thousands of promotional messages beginning with a negative. The bulk of those messages—say, 80 percent—would have been more effective if they had opened with a positive.

What about the other 20 percent? Aren't they effective? Yes, they are. But in 18 percent of the 20 percent they're a specialty, most effective when you want to initiate a reaction based on guilt, fear, or anger. Safety lies in opening with positives.

After you're under way and have built a little rapport with the reader, then it's time to push that reader through the maze of *don'ts* and *won'ts*. Use negatives to shove, to nudge, to emphasize, to add color and impact. Negatives are the seasoning. Positives are the main course.

If in four cases out of five, starting a headline with "Don't" generates antagonism or inaction, not rapport, violate that Rule with surgical care. It parallels opening one no-trump with 12 points: The bridge columnist and his partner of 30 years can do it; the social bridge player goes down three tricks for his boldness.

In power communication, generating antagonism is deadly. Worse! Reduced response, when it's the communicator's fault, is deadly.

Here are two headlines selling an office air conditioner:

- The first headline: "Don't swelter this summer."
- The second headline: "Now you can afford summer cooling."

The second headline outpulled the first, three to one. Surprising! At first glance the "Don't swelter" headline seems to be more attention-getting than the very ordinary "Now you can" headline.

On reflection, you may second-guess why the "Don't" headline hadn't pulled as well. It doesn't tell the reader to do anything. That's the "Stop" effect negatives too often have.

The Negative Bleed-Over Effect

An ad in a trade publication says, "Don't be satisfied with a development computer system until you are . . ." and it lists a group of qualifiers.

The ad itself is a fairly good piece of advertising, which makes it a perfect example of *The Rule of Negative Bleed-Over Effect:*

- The negative opening bleeds over to the reader's reaction to the advertiser.

A parenthetical tip: If you wonder whether comparative copy—that is, copy in which you compare what you sell with what a competitor sells—conforms to the Negative Bleed-Over Effect, the answer is: It certainly does.

So noninventive, hucksterish headlines such as "Don't Buy A Computer!" or "Don't Read This Ad" not only are out of fashion; they have a high damage-probability.

Don't you associate the negative opening with the company running this ad? Don't you get the impression you should be skeptical about this company? Wouldn't a positive statement be more likely to generate a positive reaction?

And don't you agree starting the first two sentences of the previous paragraph with "Don't you . . ." is more impelling than the opening of the third sentence, "Wouldn't you . . ."? We've discovered *The Negative Question Reversal:*

> ■ Opening a *question* with "Don't you" automatically sways the reader or listener toward your point of view . . . the reverse of opening a statement with "Don't."

The question reverses the negative effect, turning it into a positive.

How to Lose Sales and Alienate People

A publication placed a horribly expensive 12-page color/bleed insert in the pages of several advertising magazines.

> ■ Page 1 has a single centered word: "No."
> ■ Pages 2 and 3 have three words: "No killer bees."
> ■ Pages 4 and 5 have four words: "No freeze dried pets."
> ■ Pages 6 and 7 have three words: "No enema diets."

- Pages 8 and 9 have five words: "No eggplants that resemble politicians."
- Pages 10 and 11 have a centered heading, "None of that stuff," plus 24 reproductions of magazine covers and three paragraphs of reversed-out copy. This is the first paragraph:

No killer bees. No monkeys who can drive. No reports of Elvis at the shopping mall. None of that stuff. Between the covers of US *magazine, you'll discover the best entertainment news and information on the planet; more comprehensive than* Vanity Fair; *more focused than* People.

See what's wrong here? Telling us what the magazine *doesn't* have, this writer deals in absolute specifics. Trying to tell us what the magazine *does* have, the writer deals in thin generalities.

Too many writers who value form over substance write negative ads. Why? They're easy to do. Starting with "Don't" doesn't require a lot of thought. In a hurry to meet a deadline, or just not thinking the way a salesperson is supposed to think, the writer drives his keyboard into a hazard, *The Negative Gear-Strip Probability:*

- Because negative headlines *always* require a gearshift, getting to the point can be tortuous. The reader can't determine what the advertiser wants him to do.

Following a hard positive with a fast hard negative *isn't* so easy. When well done, it's as shrewdly motivational as any copy we'll ever see.

Our Income CD won't leave you pinched.

2 YEAR CD
7.30%
$1,000 DEPOSIT

In fact, you won't even have to tighten your belt. Because the high interest you earn is deposited into your Cal Fed checking account every month. Automatically. You don't have to think about it. It's just there. And it's safe. Because Cal Fed continues to exceed all federal regulatory capital requirements and deposits are FDIC insured. At Cal Fed, we'll make sure you don't get caught in a jam.

CAL ⚡ FED
CALIFORNIA FEDERAL BANK
FSB

1-800-341-5533 Ext. 325

FDIC Rate shown is simple interest. Substantial interest penalty for early withdrawal. Rate shown is subject to change without notice and upon renewal.

Fig. 6.1
If Cal Fed's Income CD won't leave you pinched, how will it leave you? Weak hucksterism is a common result for communications describing what <u>won't</u> happen; the message asks for attention instead of action. (An easy way to avoid hucksterism: Be sure the illustration matches the basic message, not just the headline.)

This headline has a positive quickly followed by a negative:

*NEW YORK FIRM SWEARS
ITS $5 DESIGNER BAGS
ARE NOT STOLEN*

Here we have a powerful positive—"Swears"—followed by the most dynamic negative—"Not." (For purposes of dissection forget the lack of ethics in this approach. We have to admire whoever adapted the venerable "They say I'm crazy but I'm not" theme.)

What if the writer reversed the polarity:

*$5 DESIGNER BAGS
ARE NOT STOLEN,
NEW YORK FIRM SWEARS*

No type treatment, no dependence on exclamation points could bring this surrogate to a point of equivalent strength. This is the kind of headline one finds on muckraking news stories.

What do we do about those who are annoyed, outraged, or itchy because of that word "stolen"? The advertiser's position probably is, "They wouldn't buy anyway." And "stolen" makes the negative complete, because this word itself has only negative connotations.

Negatives in Broadcast Copy

Negatives are less desirable in broadcast copy than they are in copy for print media. Why? Because the refer-back possibility doesn't exist. Listeners retain the negative because reevaluation of the spoken word requires more aggressive participation than reevaluation of the printed word.

So beginning a commercial with "Don't . . ." or "Never . . ." can be considerably more damaging than beginning a print ad with a negative word. Safer and more suitable: imperatives. (See chapter 7, "Why Imperatives Work in Broadcast Media.")

The Difference Between *Un* and *Not*

Don't use *un* and *not* interchangeably. The overtones aren't identical.

The difference between *un* and *not*: *Un* seems more inadvertent; *not* seems more intentional. *Unmarried* implies a condition existing without conscious decision making; *Not married* implies the result of a state of mind.

Similar Words with Different Implications

Choosing between words *apparently* similar can reflect a positive or negative reaction without using additional positive or negative qualifiers. **Examples:**

Positive	Negative
eager	anxious
dirty	filthy
opportunity	chance
look forward to	face

So as this book reiterates so often, synonyms aren't always synonymous. The meaning of a whole message veers obliquely with misuse.

The difference between "looking forward to" and "face" is obvious when we deliberately experiment with interchangeability: One looks forward to a weekend of playing golf and faces a weekend of painting the house.

Lots and lots of words you may have used as synonymous replacements can suffer from improper translation *in the reader's mind*: Your intended positive (or neutral) becomes negative; your intended negative (or neutral) becomes positive; your intended neutral becomes positive or negative.

Not with power communication in place! You won't use *dirty* instead of *filthy* when you want to project the most negative imagery.

You won't use *chance* instead of *opportunity* when you want to project the most positive imagery.

Best of all, you'll know when to switch so eagerness *can* become anxiety, so dirt *can* become filth, so opportunity *can* become chance:

> *This is your last chance to take advantage of this opportunity.*

How might we reverse this word use? Perhaps if we were describing a lottery:

> *This is your last opportunity to take advantage of this chance.*

Probably not. But you get the idea.

How About That Other 20%?

Please qualify this statement as the author's opinion: A negative opening can outpull a positive opening when the message-thrust leans on one of these three motivators:

1. Guilt;
2. Fear;
3. Anger.

Although it's the most forceful motivator, anger is a rarity in conventional power communication. Anger is best suited to fund raising messages aimed at co-extremists.

Two facets have to be congruent to bring a negative-based communication to white heat.

First, the illustration should match the tone. This isn't easy, but it's necessary because a negative headline and a bright, happy illustration destroy each other's impact.

Second, if the opening negative proposes a problem, the writer has to tell the reader, quickly: The purpose of this notification is to make available a solution to the problem.

A fund-raising space ad grabs *guilt* to its bosom, answering a negative perfectly with both text and picture. The entire copy:

"I can't afford the United Way this year. The kids
need new shoes."
We know.

Illustration is brilliantly conceived: a pair of scuffed children's shoes attached to fierce-looking prosthetic devices.

Should the Communicator Play It Safe?

If you're a gambler . . . if you just can't seem to get past that break-even point . . . if you're writing to a "vertical" group, catering to a single point of interest . . . if you're raising funds on a highly emotional level . . . try a negative opening. You might be one of the 20 percent.

For other circumstances, if you have a dazzling idea, follow the Yellow Brick Road: Test it.

The Connotation Rule Revisited

Exceptions are worthy of exploration, because successful exceptions are the embryo of the next mainstream.

We all know *The Connotation Rule*, one of the floor-beams under *most* force-communication because most force-communication wants to establish a mood of cheerful confidence:

- Substitute words and phrases with a positive connotation for words and phrases with a neutral or negative connotation.

We certainly know the most common negatively-connoting words and phrases. They usually have a *don't* or *can't* or *no* or *not* in them, unrelated to the central selling argument.

But within the Rule is a Pandora's Box, helpful negatives clamoring to get out: If the negative *is* related to the central selling argument, such as "Won't stain your clothes," the Rule doesn't apply. (*Won't* isn't a thorough negative, as *don't* is.) If the communication intends to frighten the reader or listener, the Rule doesn't apply.

Knowing the Rule doesn't mean we can recognize neutral words as painlessly as we recognize negative words. It's an exceptionally sticky wicket because a word which might have power in one circumstance becomes a weak sister in another.

That's why a beginning writer has no trouble replacing negatives but turns butcher by extending the scalpel to include the "good" negative words.

The Rule of Negative Transmission

The 1990s are years of stridency. Speakers stand defiantly at the rostrum, flail their arms, and pound away even when transmitting information instead of philosophy and even when addressing compatriots. Clergymen rail at those who show up for Sunday morning services because others are playing golf. Often the result is *numbness*. The person who shouts every line loses impact with each succeeding sentence.

Aggressive transmission of negative information has its place. *The Rule of Negative Transmission* covers its uses and abuses:

- Unless you want the reader or viewer to think you're the originator or generator of the reason for negative information, don't put this information aggressively.

Two Subrules of Negative Transmission

Modifying the Rule of Negative Transmission are two Subrules.

- *Subrule 1*: Don't tell the reader, "You have a problem," unless you reassure him a little later on, "but I have the solution to your problem."
- *Subrule 2*: Don't open a selling argument with "Don't." Save this word, which can kill rapport, until you've introduced a "Do . . ." for the reader to cling to.

Fig. 6.2
Negative openings can work when copy takes a sternly parental tone. This stark message might have been a father's sharp warning to his careless offspring. Effectiveness suffers some damage from the light-hearted illustration.

(A parenthetical paradox: Does this Subrule by its very wording contradict itself? No. It doesn't open the selling argument but appears properly, as a backup.)

This was the communication from an advertising trade directory:

If your firm is not listed in this directory, you are making it difficult for your customers and prospects to keep you in mind.

In the Age of Skepticism, this message is a generation out of date. The reader's reaction to this type of message has changed from, "Oh, dear," to, "Who the hell do you think you are?"

Oh, yes. Messages telling us we're failures have even greater power than they did before this Gray Age came upon us. But they're tempered by the First Subrule. Telling us we have a problem won't sell us anything unless it's accompanied by the solution.

If your foreign car is not being serviced at

FOREIGN CAR SERVICE AND PARTS
it's not being serviced!

749-9701
6520 W. Commercial Blvd. Lauderhill. ☐

Fig. 6.3
*Image advertising such as this is 40 years out-of-date. The "If . . .
not" construction seldom is the most motivational message in this
Age of Skepticism, because "If" tied to "not" implicitly avoids telling the reader what to do.*

With that mix in place, the communicator's job is to (a) convince us the problem exists; (b) convince us the solution is at hand. Is the directory a solution to a problem we didn't know we had? Tell us what the problem is . . . and how you'll solve it. Self-serving labeling doesn't convince us.

Violators of the Second Subrule often are dilettantes, beginners, or burnouts. In their desperation they use the means as an end, the "Don't . . ." phrase substituting for projection of a genuine reason to respond.

Starting a sales argument with "Don't . . ." has another problem: It's a cliché. How many ads have we seen and heard, year after year, with this type of opening: "Don't Buy a New Car . . ." or "Don't Read This Ad . . ." or "Don't Watch This Scene . . ." or "Don't listen . . ." (all followed by "unless . . ."). The writer's notion stems from a dangerous notion: Shock value stems from reinterpretation and results in the reader admiring the copy.

And so it did when this device first appeared, between the Great Wars. But we're in the Age of Skepticism. The reader comes to our messages with holster unbuttoned, waiting for us to make a false move so he or she can drill our message through its heart: "Gotcha, ya varmint!" (See "The Inversion Technique," later in this chapter.)

Fear is one of the great motivators during the Age of Skepticism, so a negative sales argument attacking the reader's failings—*provided the reader acknowledges those failings*—becomes the height of the art when coupled to a solution. A powerful ad is headed:

First you have to admit
you're impotent.

Why is it powerful? Because it leaps into the center of the problem, brushing away those to whom impotence is no problem and reassuring the reader, whose anguish existed *before* seeing this message (recognize this as a key), "We'd like to change all that."

The writer may be clever, but he doesn't call attention to cleverness by getting cute. The message is starkly commanding to its targets.

That's how a communicator accomplished in negatives takes command—by switching positions with the person who sees or hears the sales argument; then, like the anti-hero of George Orwell's "1984," saying to that person, "Here's what you fear most . . . and Big Daddy will make it well."

Use Negatives to Deny a Pejorative

How does one *deny* a pejorative? (*Pejorative* is a derogatory term, trying to make something or somebody appear to be a little worse.)

When denying a pejorative, a negative reference is stronger than a positive reference: "He was smart" is weaker than "He was no dummy."

As we communicators become increasingly fascinated by the relationship of positives and negatives, we no longer can preach a blind catechism—

- Q. Why are positives stronger than negatives?
- A. Because positives dictate action and negatives dictate inaction.

The catechism is an inadequate blanket, as the next example shows.

Suppose you insult somebody publicly. The person is a logical target—a politician or an actor or a copywriter. You say, "This guy is stupid." The knee-jerk response is, "Oh, no, he isn't"—a negative—quickly followed by the positive, "He's really bright when you get to know him."

Two options here. We can drop the negative and begin our defense with the upbeat, "He's really bright . . ."—a half-admission because it accepts the opponent's position; or we can use the detractor's own terms, a far more solid base:

"He isn't stupid at all."

The denying negative becomes positive, because it uses the detractor's own word to reverse the pejorative. This makes it stronger than a positive rebuttal, which embraces the argument without controverting.

Admitting a Deficiency . . . Gracefully

When one has to admit a deficiency and doesn't want the reader or listener to draw a totally negative conclusion, instead of "It isn't . . ." or "It doesn't . . ." substitute "It hasn't been known to . . ." or "In the past it hasn't . . ." or "Records don't indicate that . . ."

This technique—so well known to politicians—exemplifies *The Rule of Indirect Weakness:*

> ■ The less harsh and direct the message, the less powerful it is.

Indirect and mildly evasive message constructions benefit from bleaching power *out*.

The Absolute Rule of Negative References

One more rule relative to the negative imperative—*The Absolute Rule of Negative References:*

- Use a negative reference to whatever you're selling only if such a reference will help either salesworthiness, credibility, or both.

Competitors take potshots. Targets are triumphant when they find holes in a selling argument. The Absolute Rule of Negative References won't stop competitors and targets from taking aim, but it can protect a communication from shooting itself in the foot.

If you *want* to generate negative feelings, The Absolute Rule of Negative References becomes mandatory.

For fund-raisers, *The First Subrule of Absolute References* could be the most valuable of all the rules and tips in this book:

- Don't use positive words when you're trying to generate negative feelings.

Seem abstruse, especially since it begins with "Don't"? It isn't, when you apply this concept to battle-condition communications. A fund-raising letter has this line:

> *As you may know, multiple sclerosis is more than a concern to the nation's young people—it is THE #1 DISABLING DISEASE OF YOUNG ADULTS.*

How do *you* accept "#1"? Aside from the unnecessary use of the pound-mark for "number," you think positively—"the #1 car dealer," "the #1 seller," "ranked #1 in actual taste tests."

As a private game, rewrite this sentence using a *negative* reference to replace *#1*.

What alternative did you come up with? "Deadliest . . ."? "Far and away most lethal . . ."? Whatever your replacement, if the words match the negative image you're trying to create you're more likely to induce the proper reaction.

Matching the Negative Image

Just as *deadliest* describes a disease better than *#1*, so does "We won't forget" describe a commitment *related to a negative circumstance* better than "We'll always remember."

So "We'll never forget," followed by a negative, can reach deeper into the reader's subconscious than "We'll always remember" . . . *if* the episode is itself negative. For a funeral oration, "We'll never forget." For a rally celebrating a football victory, "We'll always remember."

Negative Conditional to Show the Upper Limit of Positive

Use a negative conditional (*could*) reference to show a positive at its upper limit:

They couldn't have been more accommodating.

Careful! The same construction can show a negative at its lower limit. This is something of a paradox, because in this usage the line separating negatives and positives becomes blurred:

- I couldn't care less.
- He couldn't eat one more bite.

Less **Is Usually Negative**

When you use the word *less*, *double-check* your copy for negative implications.

The difference between these sentences can be the difference between making a sale, or not:

- You pay considerably less for your subscription.
- Others pay considerably more for their subscriptions.

When *Less* is the opening gun in a sales argument, the word can fleetingly suggest the reader *gets* less. "You get your subscription at a far lower rate . . ." avoids the construction altogether.

The word *less* gathers power to itself when you *want* to project a negative. Be sure less is more.

". . . less" As a Suffix

Flawless is a positive word. Or is it?

In usage, it's absolutely positive. For generations we've accepted "flawless diamond" as *more* positive than "perfect diamond." But other ". . . less" words can cause more comprehension problems than they solve. Among those words:

artless	nameless
blameless	nerveless
ceaseless	profitless
faithless	selfless
faultless	sunless
guiltless	timeless
joyless	tuneless
matchless	

The problem doesn't exist for words which through usage have lost their "less" meaning. Some are positive—

deathless	noiseless
fearless	priceless

and some are negative, but without a true "deficiency/'less'" significance (compared with *more*)—

defenseless	mindless
endless	penniless
fruitless	senseless
helpless	thankless
homeless	thoughtless
merciless	worthless

A few of these words have ". . .ful" positive parallels—*fruitful/fruitless, merciful/merciless, thoughtful/thoughtless*—but *mindful* has no relationship with *mindless* and *helpful* isn't the reverse of *helpless*.

The suffix "less" *usually* suggests something is missing. This gives it a connotation different from conventional negatives. "Drip-less" isn't as effective a description of a faucet as "no-drip" or "never-drip." The "less" suffix becomes valuable when the writer wants the reader to consider whatever is missing not as a deficiency but as a change or aberration: "He's heartless" has considerably more impact than "He has no heart."

Using "less" words to emphasize anger, fear, guilt, or despair can have an impact positive words don't have. Why? Because positive words generate an upbeat reaction.

Yes.
Yes.
Yes.

NCNB's LineOne® Equity Loan Offer Has Been Extended.

Yes, NCNB's special LineOne Equity offer is now available until April 15, 1991. **Yes,** that means no closing costs or annual fees.* And, **Yes,** you can use your LineOne Equity line of credit on anything from home improvement to college education, even to buy a car. And you still may be able to take advantage of some tax-saving benefits. Consult your tax advisor to find out how it could best help you and how limitations on deductibility apply. Then consult NCNB at **1-800-283-NCNB** to find out more about LineOne Equity loans. You never know, this could be the answer you've been waiting for.

NCNB
LineOne®Equity

*LineOne Equity is available on only one- to four-family primary residences, including condominiums. Your loan will be secured by a mortgage (lien) on your home. The variable Annual Percentage Rate (APR) will be the latest Prime Rate as published in The Wall Street Journal plus 2% (13.0% APR as of 4/1/91). Rates may increase to 18%. Apart from this rate cap, there is no limit on the amount by which the rate may increase. Property Insurance may be required. LineOne Equity cannot be used to purchase a residence or for any commercial purposes. NCNB National Bank of Florida. Member FDIC. © 1991 NCNB Corporation.

⌂ Equal Housing Lender. No closing costs in a limited-time offer. Closing costs offer good through April 15, 1991.

Fig. 6.4
Which of these two ads is more likely to generate a phone call to the bank? Unquestionably the "No, No, No" ad is provocative, especially with the doubled negative subhead—"With NCNB's Line One® Equity Loan, These May Be The Best Words You Hear." But

"No, No, No."

With NCNB's LineOne® Equity Loan, These May Be The Best Words You Hear.

No, we will not charge you closing costs. **No,** there will not be annual fees. And, **No,** tax-deductibility is not a thing of the past. Yes, you heard right. With NCNB's LineOne Equity you can take advantage of getting a personal line of credit to use for anything from home improvement to college education, even to buy a car. And still be able to take advantage of tax-saving benefits. Consult your tax advisor to find out how it could best help you and how limitations on deductibility apply. Then consult NCNB at **1-800-283-NCNB** to find out more about LineOne Equity loans. You never know, it could be the answer you've been waiting for.

NCNB
LineOne Equity

a classic rule of force-communication is: Getting attention is not parallel to offering a benefit. Demanding a total re-evaluation midway through the advertisement typifies messages whose intention is to startle rather than motivate.

The Difference Between "If You're Not" and "If You Aren't"

The difference between "If you're not . . ." and "If you aren't . . ." lies in the degree of negativism generated by the controlling word—*not* or *are*.

This is one of those dinky little power improvers. You may use it twice in your lifetime, or you may opt for permanent adoption. "If you're not . . ." accents the word *not*; "If you aren't . . ." accents the word *are*. So "If you're not . . ." is more negative than "If you aren't . . ."

Don't believe it? Try it. Write out a complete sentence using each one. The "aren't" version is softer, less dynamic. This suggests the comparative value of each version when making the choice: Do you want to be emphatic or subdued?

The "Inversion Technique": A Shopworn Gauntlet

In the 1930s and 1940s some advertisers thought it was cute to invert a sales message so it was negative instead of positive—"Don't Read This Ad . . ."; "Why You Shouldn't Buy at Smith's"; "A Dozen Reasons Why Shoppers Avoid Us." The idea was to startle us into reading the message by fashioning what appeared to be an outrageous or self-deprecating message.

Hold it! We've come hurtling through future shock and have bounced twice at the far end. This type of ad is about as startling as "Why does a chicken cross the road?"

But we still see it in print. A writer, slightly out of phase with today's seller-sellee relationships, uses the tired Inversion Technique.

How many times have you seen space ads with a huge headline—"Don't Buy a New Car!"—followed by the trite, barf-bait line, ". . . Until you've seen the 1993 Whatever." Don't you feel a little insulted, without analyzing why?

An admonition doesn't make friends for you, and coupled with a cliché it can be deadly. A company selling business lists ran a space ad headed:

*"Don't Monkey Around
with a Monster Like . . .
DIRECT CONNECTION
LIST & PACKAGE INSERT PROGRAM*

The illustration? An ape. Clever, huh?

Whatever the ad means, in this author's opinion the writer made a monkey out of himself. The writer could have made an asset out of himself by avoiding the pitfall word "Don't" as the trigger.

It's easy to write an inverted ad. All you have to do is, with whatever tongue-in-cheek talent you may have, suggest to the reader that he *not* buy from you.

The reader is supposed to say, "What a clever fellow that writer is."

You lose both ways. If the reader doesn't say it, your wit isn't as projectible as you thought it was. If he does say it, you've violated one of the great laws of force-communication:

*In this Age of Skepticism, cleverness for the sake of
cleverness may well be a liability rather than an asset.*

So a coupon ad with an inverted headline is neither startling nor titillating. The headline:

6 reasons for not *sending*
for absolutely Free *details about*
the Home Business Directory

We beat this approach about the head and shoulders not because of blind prejudice against the Inversion Technique . . . not because it isn't ever possible to use a negative effectively, as this very chapter points out . . . but because whoever wrote this ad cheated whoever hired him or her by delivering a less effective message than was so readily at hand.

So starting a sales argument with "Don't" has three important objections going against it:

1. It's dangerous psychology;
2. It's a cliché;
3. It's often sophomoric.

Controlling the Degree of Negativism

The communicator controls the degree of negativism through word choice. The next three statements are negatives; the degrees of negativism aren't the same.

In order, with most positive first:

- It may or may not be that . . .
- It's debatable whether . . .
- It's questionable whether . . .

Advocate? Dispassionate observer? Antagonist? Each of these masks attitude *slightly* while projecting viewpoint.

Softening the Negative: "Not Exactly"

The word *exactly*, after *not*, adds a disarming wryness and softens the negative: "Our team is not exactly Super Bowl quality."

Look at the difference between the harsh "Our team isn't Super Bowl quality" and the ironic "Our team is not exactly Super Bowl quality." If you want a heaping teaspoon of irony, underline or italicize "exactly": "Our team is not *exactly* Super Bowl quality."

What this does is parallel, in writing, the interpretive dominance a speaker has. The speaker can deliver the identical statement three or four different ways. His listeners know exactly how he meant it. Have you ever been interviewed by a semihostile reporter and seen some of your own words in print? Without inflection and emphasis, your words can parallel the old Yiddish joke:

> *Prosecutor: Did you steal a chicken?*
> *Accused: (in Yiddish) I stole a chicken?*
> *Translator: Your honor, he says he stole a chicken.*

One of the more immediate benefits the power communicator enjoys is being able to parallel in print a reader reaction the speaker can generate by voice. *Exactly* is one of our gimmicks.

Examples Are More Positive Than Statistics

Replacing a statistic with an example or a testimonial eliminates a possible negative reaction. **Example:**

Eighty percent of our buyers buy again.

or—

Eight of ten buyers buy again.

The reader's reaction: What about the other 20%?

Avoid the possible negative altogether with, "I bought. Yes, of course I'll buy again." (See *The Rule of Statistical Deficiency*, chapter 2.)

Positive Selection of Details

Select details that sell without potentially generating a negative. Example of a gratuitously generated negative:

Insert the batteries. You won't have to replace them for two years.

Two negatives here: First, the word *insert* suggests, however mildly, the necessity of work. Second, the entire statement points out the need to replace the batteries.

The "In . . ." and "Im . . ." Negative Prefix

"In" or "im"—meaning *not*—doesn't plaster as permanent a tag on its subject as *not*.

Knowing this gives us a little more control over the degree of negativism we project. **For example:**

Condition may be temporary	*Condition is permanent*
inconvenient	not convenient
inconsistent	not consistent
inoperative	not operational
inappropriate	not appropriate
incapable	not capable
immaterial	not material
immature	not mature
immodest	not modest
immoral	not moral

My explanation may have muddied this point by trying to clarify it. In some cases, the actual word might change. For example, for *inconsistent* a communicator might substitute *erratic*. But try emphasizing by underlining, italicizing, or verbal stress. "In" or "im" can't handle it: *Im*modest looks artificial, drawing attention to your emphasis device rather than to the intended effect. *Not* is problem-free: *Not* modest is pure subject-emphasis.

Making the Message Recipient Your Partner: The Agreement-Seeking Question

Too many communications—especially those from companies with a bad case of unwitting corporate arrogance—annoy the message-recipient by an assumption of acceptance: "Of course you want to do business with us."

A dangerous game! An oh-so-easy way to avoid sandpapering the recipient's ego is *The Agreement-Seeking Question Rule:*

- Adding an agreement-seeking question to the end of a claim makes the reader your partner.

A letter opens this way:

*I'm counting on your being the type of executive I
think you are. You'll certainly be kind enough to
acknowledge receipt of this letter.*

Typical, but unnecessarily risky. Let's make this communication less imperious by the simple addition of a two-word question:

*I'm counting on your being the type of executive I
think you are. You'll certainly be kind enough to
acknowledge receipt of this letter—won't you?*

Fewer hackles rise. The reader is the writer's partner. Asking
for logical agreement has this big benefit: *The reader is more likely
to accept what you say as logical.*

So instead of writing—

It's the only way to fly.

we write—

It's the only way to fly, isn't it?

The agreement-seeking question opens with a positive statement . . . and the positive statement directs the answer. "Is this
yours?" is 50/50: It doesn't ask for a yes or a no. "This is yours,
isn't it?" is 80/20: It directs the answer.

Without the positive opening, the question is less directional.
"Isn't this better?" doesn't lead the reaction as strongly as "This
is better, isn't it?"

Shooting Yourself in the Foot Means "Ouch!"

Joining the Inversion Technique in obnoxious negativism is an anachronism, a holdover from the 1950s and 60s. Some marketers still believe they can compete by acknowledging the superiority of competitors or by exposing their own weaknesses, like an impotent "flasher."

Our competitors are delighted to point out our weaknesses and shortcomings. Why should we join them?

This isn't a school of communications. It's a kindergarten of communications, believing in the "confessional" doctrine that total disclosure is better for us than promotional self-serving non-messages.

Maybe so, in the cosmic scheme of things; but we'll never sell more by artless candor than by selective use of fact.

A mailing from an envelope company, headed "YOU GET WHAT YOU PAY FOR," begins its short message with these first two sentences:

> *What good are low prices if your envelopes are not*
> *there when needed???*
> *Our prices may be higher, but we guarantee delivery*
> *when* <u>you need it</u>*!!*

The multiple punctuation marks and strange decision to underline "you need it" but not "when" suggest a semi-pro approach; but what benefit does the phrase "Our prices may be higher" add? Opinion: This mailing shoots itself in the foot.

An even more self-destructive example:

Fig. 6.5
Why lead the reader in a negative direction? As an opening, a negative requires considerable text to turn around the reader's or listener's assumption.

© 1992 The Dartnell Corporation

Which would you rather have?
Low prices or genuine service and attention?
If you're smart enough to want service,
this is the place.

Not just the foot. This one blows away every organ south of the navel.

Using Negatives to Transmit a Warning

When transmitting a warning or caution, negatives can be stronger than positives because they inject fear into the motivational mix.

"Your radar detector won't gradually lose battery power" emphasizes danger and, so, has greater wallop than "Your radar detector maintains full battery power," which emphasizes the status quo.

Don't Lapse Into Weak Negatives

Changing a negative to a positive can make a prosaic line exciting. Most readers wouldn't find fault with this line:

That's a marvelously low price, but it isn't all I have
for you today.

The line transmits information clearly and efficiently; but would it have taken any longer to squeeze off a little shot of excitement, a tiny barb added to the bullet?

That's a marvelously low price, but I have even better
news for you today.

What's the difference in impact? 20%? 10%? 1%? However fractional it is, why not take advantage of it? That's why communicators either can claim power or ignore it.

The Negative Hedge

A negative statement can be a hedge: "Our planet isn't flat," opposed to "Our planet is round"; "Don't make a mistake," opposed to "Make no mistake"; "Alzheimer's isn't irreversible,"opposed to "Alzheimer's is reversible."

You can see the value of the hedge: The reader is less likely to think you're starting an argument and less likely to retort, "No it isn't."

Beyond that, the negative hedge can actually be more positive than a hard affirmative statement:

"In that costume, she was not ignored" makes a more definite point than, "In that costume, she was noticed." Underlining the negative enhances the effect: "In that costume, she was <u>not</u> ignored."

Hard, Medium, and Soft *No*

The word *No* is absolute.

It's the first word we learn in a foreign language; it's usually the first comprehensible word a baby hears from its mother. *No* has no shades of meaning.

Having no shades of meaning is valuable, because no one can misunderstand the message. But in power communication, we sometimes want to say no . . . without the unconditional mantle of harshness. In such circumstances, "I think not" is a logical substitute.

When you don't want to issue a hard *No* but want your position understood as unshakable, try "I think not." If you want to leave the door open, a better line is "I don't think so."

"I think not" and "I don't think so" aren't parallel. The first expression begins with *think*, a mild positive, and ends with *not*, a clear negative; "I don't think so" begins with *don't*, a clear negative, and ends with *so*, a positive.

Speaking of *no*, its very harshness lends it extra strength when describing product ingredients.

When you want to show exclusion, *no* is stronger than "free of." Example: "No cholesterol" and "no fat" make a stronger statement than "cholesterol-free" and "fat-free"; but for emphasis, add typographic treatment—"*no* fat." This can't work with *free*— "fat-*free*" makes interpretation more difficult.

The Difference Between "Didn't Ask" and "Haven't Asked"

The difference between "didn't ask" and "haven't asked" is a microcosm of the whole concept of power communication.

A distributor writes a sales letter to the buyer at a chain of retail stores, or his representative calls on that buyer. Written or verbal, the difference between two ways of couching the same information registers on the brain of the message recipient.

That individual may not recognize his or her own reaction— the words influenced a state of mind. *That's* Power Persuasion!

The salesperson says, mailing or handing samples to the buyer:

I know you didn't ask for these samples.

or—

I know you haven't asked for these samples.

The difference is the natural difference between *did not* and *have not*. *Did not* = could have asked, made a deliberate negative choice. *Have not* = possibly motivated, possibly unmotivated; lack of action might stem from the individual's lack of knowledge.

A second cousin to this point is the difference between *not any* and *no*. *Not any* is more decisive than *no*. Example: "I don't see any problem" bestows more authority to the message transmitter than "I see no problem."

The Difference Between "We're Not" and "We Aren't"

As communications engineers, our hands have to be firmly on the throttle of our rhetorical locomotives.

When we round a curve, we don't want to keep that throttle wide open. We can derail our message.

That's the benefit of knowing the difference between "we're not" and "we aren't." "We're not" is stronger, more potent, lightly brushed with an acid coat, suggesting whatever we're not is either (a) by our choice or (b) annoying to us. "We aren't" is bland and unvarnished. For example, "We're not staying"—a position—or "We aren't staying"—a simple declarative. "We're not going to lose this game" is Knute Rockne at halftime; "We aren't going to lose this game" is a hope.

The greatest value of the difference between the two phrases occurs when a *noun* follows:

We're not the ones you're looking for.

or—

We aren't the ones you're looking for.

We're not a bunch of murderers.

or—

We aren't a bunch of murderers.

We're not babies.

or—

We aren't babies.

Don't read viewpoint into this interpretation. The difference gives us ammunition *both ways*. We can avoid subliminal irritation just as readily as we can stimulate it.

But as a Negative/Positive

This book is peppered with the word *but*. (See Chapter 3, "No Buts About It," describing the word as a condition changer.) Logical enough: It's loaded with warnings.

"But" *as a transition* is usually negative. If you want to soften the message, use *though*; if you want the transition to be neutral, use "and"; if you want it to be positive, use "so."

But—because "but" is a condition changer, we have to include it here as well as Chapter 3, because the word reverses the previous thought.

When you want to scare or warn your target . . . and then soften or solve the problem or add the dimension of hope . . . "but" is the word. Two negatives = a positive. That's the logic behind using "but" after a negative statement; your reader or listener *knows* from the word itself that what follows will reverse the original negative.

Are we saying our prices have been higher and we've lowered them? Not at all. Does the reader interpret our words to mean our prices were higher and we've lowered them? Very possibly.

The Benefit of Knowing When to Do and When to Don't

In the last decade of the 20th century, most messages from commercial sources are saturated with "hype." Response from target individuals gets weaker and weaker—in ratio to the realization that positives originating in puffery are really just hype.

This gives the power communicator a more cosmic view of negatives. The recognition:

On some occasions negatives have a more positive emotional effect than a flat positive, because skeptics find a negative statement less assailable.

To the professional communicator, negatives can be an exquisite spice, flavoring the communications-mixture and making it more palatable to the recipient.

Chapter 7
Power Communication Through Throwaways

Thoughtlessness may be the number one reason for professional communications failure.

When a professional athlete, who has golden hands with a basketball but base metal in communications skills, lards statements with "Y'know" and "I mean" and "Like," we accept the deficiency without judgment. We don't look to most athletes for verbal or written information.

The professional communicator doesn't have this excuse. The working muscles in brain and fingertips have to be as highly developed as the arm-muscles of a basketball player. Otherwise, the host of critics who look for reasons to attack advertising messages get a little more justification.

The power communicator stays in control. A throwaway phrase? If thrown, we have a reason. Isn't leaving interpretation to chance as unprofessional as not knowing the rules at all?

Throwaway phrases have greater significance in spoken communication than in written communication. This is because their function as tempering devices can be emphasized or diminished by inflection.

So included in this chapter are suggested word uses for broadcast communication—radio, in which sound is the only communicator; and television, in which sound explains, flavors, leavens, and/or reinterprets visual imagery.

A "Throwaway" Example:
Confusing Geography with Sourcing

Let's start with a tough example:

*Unless you specifically want to suggest geography,
don't use terminology which confuses geography with
sourcing.*

This one may seem confusing, but that's only because of the
difficulty of condensing this point into a few words. An example
will clarify:

This exclusive offer is not available anywhere else.

The seeds are here, but the word "anywhere" can have two
meanings:

1. We're the only source;
2. Those in other geographic areas can't (a) offer it or
   (b) have access to it.

Who needs even a touch of confusion? We restructure the
sentence to read—

This exclusive offer is available only from us.

The meaning is unmistakable. Incidentally, if you're aching
to inject a *you* or two into this thought, professionalism is on your
side . . . provided the structure is reworded. "This exclusive offer
is available to you only from us" generates another problem: The
reader may feel it's available to others from another source.

Before You Throw It Away, Ask Yourself: Will It Irritate Some Target-Prospects?

Careful, careful, with words that by their very nature will irritate some of the people you want to influence.

The writer whose letter, selling porcelain figurines, used the phrase "hard-core collector," knows what this caution means. A lot of readers over age 55 see those words *hard-core* and reach a set-in-cement conclusion about the morality of the unwitting figurine source.

Instead of arguing semantics, why take this risk? When the author saw a mailer from a syndicated creative source his own attitude took even sharper form. A key sentence from this mailer:

We make up a new ad each month and strip your name in it.

The negative reaction to the word *strip* is a mechanical one. No one wants to be part of a creative cattle-call, and this copy emphasizes the target's anonymity instead of massaging the target's ego. Too, others might reach a different but equally negative subliminal conclusion about the word. Why not *print* or *include* the name in it instead of stripping it in?

Completely off this point: Dear Creative Source, use some of your sparkling creativity on your own copy and rewrite your sentence to read something like this: "Every month you'll get a new ad—with *your* name custom-printed in it."

Good, Better, and *Best*

Good, better, and *best* not only demand validation (in some instances under prodding of government regulatory agencies), they often are communication-weakeners because they're the least specific of all the comparative words.

An over-the-counter pharmaceutical had this throwaway line:

What makes Glofirm better than old-fashioned remedies is its better formulation.

Information transmitted: Zero. The fault lies squarely on the sloping shoulders of the word "better," which adds nothing to the comprehensional mix. (See "Comparatives," chapter 8.) Generally, unproved comparatives are weakeners because they transmit no information.

A suggestion: After writing a piece of copy, let your search key become your search-and-destroy key. Even the mildest rewrite improves the Glofirm copy:

What makes Glofirm more effective than old-fashioned remedies is its special fast-dissolving formulation.

"Cop-Out" Statements

"Cop-out" statements exemplify the difference between *throwaway* as a single word and *throw away* as two words.
Cop-outs aren't throwaways; *throw* cop-outs *away*. Cop-out statements by their very nature are vague, self-serving, and often untrue.

What's a cop-out statement? Here are a few:

- Research tells us that . . .
- It is estimated that . . .
- It has been established that . . .
- For a great many reasons . . .

- A great man once said . . .
- Many agree that . . .
- Certain factors make it imperative that . . .
- Certain [circumstances, situations, events, materials] will cause a reaction that . . .
- It's important to remember that . . .
- It very well might have been that . . .

The word *that* (or, if you're a *that*-dropper, a place where the word might be) usually caps off the cop-out. What we're doing is trying to have our speculation masquerade as fact. We don't have the guts to make the flat claim, so we join B.S. Anonymous and make the same statement without worrying about getting nailed for phoniness. We attribute an opinion, masquerading as fact, to an Unidentified Authority.

The Unidentified Authority: Pros and Cons

We shouldn't use an Unidentified Authority when an identifiable authority or flat fact exists. That kind of use is unnecessary dependence.

But *necessary* dependence—ahhh! Every professional communicator has sat bemused at the keyboard, wondering how to claim superiority without the support of evidence. In those circumstances, if we can't lean on an Unidentified Authority, we can't claim superiority at all—and what kind of world would *that* be?

Unidentified Authorities should parallel that extra mini tank some mopeds have. You're out of gas, but a tiny switch releases an emergency reserve, enough to get you home.

Let Unidentified Authorities be your emergency reserve, not

Now the international business package has as many ways to go as the business person.

| WORLDPOST FIRST CLASS $11.50 | WORLDPOST BUSINESS CLASS $7.00 | WORLDPOST COACH CLASS $2.85 | WORLDPOST ECONOMY CLASS $.50* |

Some world travelers need to reach their destinations immediately—at any cost. Others have more time and options, so they can save money. Your international letters and packages really aren't much different.

WORLDPOST™ services from the U.S. Postal Service is the only carrier that gives you eight shipping options, with everything from the fastest way to send a message to the least expensive way. So whether you need to get something overseas—overnight—or have time to spare, there's a way to get it there at some of the lowest prices around.

WORLDPOST services. No one gives you more ways to go. For our free guide, call 1-800-456-3600. Or send your name and address to: WORLDPOST Services, United States Postal Service, PO Box 7899, Mt Prospect IL 60056-7899.

Circle 45 on Info Card

 **WORLDPOST**
UNITED STATES POSTAL SERVICE

U S A
OFFICIAL SPONSOR

*Prices reflect sample rates for Express Mail International Service™; International Priority Airmail™; International Surface Air Lift™; and Airmail. Effective 2/4/91. © 1991 USPS   36 USC 380

Fig. 7.1
This advertisement by the United States Postal Service is aimed at business mailers. Note the disparity between the illustration and the facts. The biggest problem, however, is the suggestion in the headline that a mailer has four options in sending the same business package—obviously not true.

your main flow. Save them for puzzling assignments with no apparent grabber-handles.

Why? Because *any* other use of an Unidentified Authority is an admission of creative defeat. As you hit the keyboard, you tell yourself (and your more critical message recipients): "I had a stronger sales argument, but I didn't bother to find it."

A writer for an investment service had this line:

> *Analysts with an enviable reputation* [unidentified] *prepare your portfolio.*

And a writer's misunderstanding of motivators resulted in excreting this sentence:

> *Dozens of people* [unidentified] were involved in bringing this to you.

On the other hand, the writer who used this Unidentified Authority showed a perverse inventiveness:

> *Rumor has it that automobile insurance rates are going up here. It isn't because of any claims you filed. It's those other drivers who aren't as careful as you.*

Who's the Unidentified Authority? A rumor.

When should you positively not use an Unidentified Authority? You positively *shouldn't* use an Unidentified Authority under two circumstances:

1. When an actual person, group, or validating fact is available.
2. When using an Unidentified Authority results in attributing an opinion or factor to the wrong source.

"Very Well": A Free Dose of Positivism

Preceding a "might" statement with "very well" adds a free dose of positivism without changing the factual core. "We very well might be there" makes it more likely that we'll be there than "We might be there."

" 'David and Goliath' very well might be the most desirable pewter sculpture our gallery—or anyone—has ever made available to you at this price." The "very well" additive adds about 20% affirmative to a fence-straddling statement. On a see-saw, 20% tips the balance.

When we can't claim a fact, adding "very well" helps our half-assertion and still insulates us against a skeptic's or competitor's or opponent's aggressive charge: "You said . . ."

Should "very well" *follow* "might"? Grammatically, why not? But we're *power* communicators, and the first impression—*might*—creates a conditional response to "very well." If the reader first sees "very well," his eye has a more optimistic view of *might*.

A Useful Throwaway Word: *Relatively*

To preserve verisimilitude when you need a hedge, keep the word *relatively* in your communications toolbox.

Relatively gives you the hedge when what you say wouldn't be true without a qualifier.

Examples:
- This process is relatively new.
- The instructions are relatively simple.
- Mileage is relatively high.

- This dress is relatively inexpensive.
- Power communications is a relatively useful concept.

The benefit of *relatively* is its "nondescriptness"—if such a word exists. The communicator can use it without challenge, except by the most determined antagonist. (And what the heck, that guy wouldn't buy from us anyway.)

What If a Word Has Multiple Meanings?

Use words which have a multiplicity of meanings at your own peril. Don't assume the reader will understand *which* way you've used a word. Murphy's Law surely will intercede against you. If the reader *can* misinterpret, the reader *will* misinterpret, so don't give your target ammunition. (See The Self-Serving Reader Rule, in this chapter.)

An example is the phrase "used to." Harmless? Not if we start compiling how many interpretations we can give this innocent phrase. An example from a catalog of consumer electronics:

This amplifier used to strengthen the signal . . .

Yes, we can agree it's out of context; in exchange, do you agree it isn't the clearest way to project a sales point? Does it mean:

    a. The amplifier strengthened the signal in times past? or
    b. This is the purpose of the amplifier? or
    c. Others have employed the amplifier to strengthen the signal?

It *could* be any.

Interpretation starts in the hands of the writer, and it should stay there. The reader can't misinterpret if the words are changed a little:

Use this amplifier to strengthen the signal . . .

or, if the product sheet dictates, the other approach:

Engineers used to select this amplifier to strengthen the signal. Now they select it for [WHATEVER].

We can't even count the number of words in our language that can be nouns, verbs, or adjectives. What we can do is clarify our own use of those words.

Whose Multiple Meaning? Ours or Theirs?

When using words with multiple meanings, avoid grief by remembering *The Self-Serving Reader Rule*:

- Assume the reader will interpret a word in its most common meaning, especially if the interpretation benefits the reader or lowers your image.

The Age of Skepticism is no time to get tricky. One reason grammarians usually are poor force-communicators is their love of language use. We, who know the value of vocabulary *suppression*, know there's little point in walking along the third rail by using words our readers might throw right back at us.

We read with horror these words extolling a major hotel:

The Executive Club pretends to be consistent with the high standards of our hotels. . . .

Deep in Webster's catacomb lurks a possible excuse for "pretends" in this usage. It's "to put in a claim; allege a title," paralleling the pretenders to the long-vanished thrones of Europe. But what in heaven's name possessed this writer? Without shifting a gear he or she could have written, "The Executive Club is proudly consistent with . . ." or "The Executive Club symbolizes . . ." or *any* word construction which doesn't suggest the Club is trying to appear better than it actually is.

Specific Throwaways

Use *Are,* Not *Remain*

"I am . . ." and "We are . . ." are more direct and more dynamic than "I remain" or "We remain."

No, this doesn't refer to an antiquated letter signoff ("I remain your dedicated servant, sir . . ."). This refers to *copy*—"We remain Mill City's leading insurance underwriter," or, "I remain the only source of discount photocopier paper."

Remain is one of those words to be used cautiously, because it's static. *We're* and *I'm* are direct and unequivocal.

How About "Plus" Instead of "And"?

Another rhetorical pebble added to the pile:

Debaters with accountant or solicitor mentalities look for pages . . . or at least paragraphs . . . or at least sentences . . . or at least multisyllabic words . . . to generate an effect. We communicators know better. Persuasion can stem from a single one-syllable word.

For example, Use *plus* instead of *and* to add emphasis. "We'll show an improvement in response . . . and an increase in the *caliber* of response" makes a clear statement. But it isn't as dynamic as the same statement with *plus* substituting for *and*: "We'll show an improvement in response . . . plus an increase in the *caliber* of response."

Let's move the italics to our key word. The differential is even stronger.

- Version A: "We'll show an improvement in response . . . *and* an increase in the caliber of response."
- Version B: "We'll show an improvement in response . . . *plus* an increase in the caliber of response."

For maximum impact, one would italicize *plus* and *caliber*. Or should we say, for maximum impact one should italicize *plus* . . . plus *caliber*?

Have vs. *Have Got*

Adding *got* to "I have" or "we have" makes the phrase more convivial and explosive, less dignified and upscale.

Of course, we wouldn't write, "We have got"; it's "We've got." Many polished writers detest and don't use this device, but no one can argue with the injection of dynamic personalization it gives a message. *Got* emphasizes *possession*, which generates a reaction to what appears to be singularity.

So the song "I Got Rhythm" can immortalize itself as "I Have Rhythm" never could. "I have an idea" suggests a more thoughtful background than "I've got an idea."

Of Course Use "Of Course"

Take another look at the first two words of the second paragraph under the previous subhead: "Of course." The statement hangs together without that phrase, so why use it?

"Of course" is a near-perfect throwaway. It's a deliberate weakener, an admission that either (a) your statement should be obvious to the message recipient or (b) you want the message recipient to know the statement is a throwaway.

Those who interview hapless candidates for jobs look for phrases such as "Of course . . ." or "Naturally . . ." If you're the applicant, use these in an interview and the pencil scribbles madly: This applicant is unsure of himself. Not executive material.

Exactly. That's the benefit reserved for those who know when to interject these softeners.

When you're pitching for business, "Of course" can be a rapport enhancer because it *doesn't* imply an Olympian position:

> *Of course you already have coverage for your car or cars . . . but of course you're interested in getting as much for your auto insurance dollar as you possibly can.*

Compare the sales wording with the identical message, lacking "Of course":

> *You already have coverage for your car or cars . . . but you're interested in getting as much for your auto insurance dollar as you possibly can.*

The difference is profound. Instead of acknowledging the reader's situation, we're casting thunderbolts from Mount Olympus. The reader can build a resentment barrier without even knowing why.

Even **Isn't Odd**

Up to this point in this chapter the word *even* has appeared six times (excluding the subhead). *Even* is a valuable throwaway. The word adds uniqueness to your offer.

For extra octane, replace "We'll refund the cost of shipping" with "We'll even refund the cost of shipping."

Even also isolates an episode and makes it singular: "[Even] in these difficult times, we're determined to maintain our entire dealer network."

"Somebody Special"

When you're looking for rapport and conviviality, a minor word change makes you a regular guy.

The subhead is "somebody special." It could have been "someone special"; *somebody* was the choice instead of *someone* because *somebody* is less formal—in fact, more coarse, a little more verbal, a little more convivial.

A good politician, in a speech, will use *anybody* and *somebody*. An invitation to join the Opera Society will use *anyone* and *someone*. The differences aren't major, but considering what you're writing, and to whom, will add an extra touch of congruency to your wording.

Coarse verbalisms have more power than sedate terminology; on the other hand, they have lower status. Don't choose the word based on personal prejudice; choose the word based on the effect you're trying to generate.

Here's a mini-list of this type of word use:

- anybody (instead of anyone)
- somebody (instead of someone)
- asked for (instead of requested)
- get (instead of receive)
- have to (instead of must)
- maybe (instead of perhaps)
- buy (instead of purchase)

If you want your words to reflect your "regular guy" image, start compiling your own list of convivialities. Nothing to it: Just write the way you talk. (If when you talk you start sentences with the word "Indeed," let us all know so we can miss your next speech.)

From and *Between*: Sometimes Surplus

Use the "search" key to ferret out surplus uses of *from* and *between*. Eliminating *from* and *between* seems to add specificity.

Examples:

A single board has from 80 to 120 chips.

replaced by—

A single board has 80 to 120 chips.

Our typical subscriber is between 35 and 54 years old.

replaced by—

Our typical subscriber is 35 to 54 years old.

The underlying concept: Qualifiers are weakeners. Technically, *from* and *between* aren't qualifiers; but in perception they are, because they add what seems to be a march-in-place moment to a declaration.

If You're One, I'm One Too

While we're feathering our communications nest, here's another:

One way to get the reader's interest in a communication is to suggest, "You're one . . . and I'm one too." Saying, "You're one," *without* adding, "I'm one too," is a dangerous game, because the writer then is throwing accusations at the reader.

But a caution—for clarity, separate the "we" linking the reader with you the writer, and "we" meaning whoever is making the offer. Analyze this paragraph, which may seem to be a perfectly logical way to sell a subscription renewal:

> ComputerPro *is right on top of the fast-paced,*
> fast-*changing world of professional computing. You*
> *and I are technicians . . . and we're businesspeople.*
> ComputerPro *is the one publication that covers both*
> *sides.*

The next paragraph reveals the communications problem:

> *We're not only packing every issue with information*
> *aimed at you, the professional; we're increasing the*
> *number of issues from four to six a year.*

All right, who are "we"? In the first paragraph, "we" are reader and writer, coupled by a common profession. In the very next paragraph, "we" are the staff at the magazine. Oh, yes, some readers may follow the transition, but other readers may *not*. Why chance confusion?

Avoiding confusion is as easy as taking one of the references out of the "we" frame. My choice is the second, because connection with the reader is more powerful than connections within the publication. So we have this minor change:

> ComputerPro *is right on top of the fast-paced,* fast-*changing world of professional computing. You and I are technicians . . . and we're businesspeople. Here is the one publication that covers both sides.*
> ComputerPro *is not only packing every issue with information aimed at you, the professional;* ComputerPro *is increasing the number of issues from four to six a year.*

In *any* communication, recognize the dominance of The Clarity Commandment, repeated here because of its relevance to every message we write or speak:

> *In force-communication, clarity is paramount. Don't let any other component of the communications mix interfere with it.*

The Adjectival Pitfall

The Adjectival Pitfall can damage an otherwise serviceable piece of copy.

What's the Adjectival Pitfall? It's the interjection of an adjec-

tive where you don't need one. The adjective either (a) weakens
or (b) changes the impact of your message.

Example: Suggested envelope copy for a worthy fund-raising
enterprise had this wording:

Because of you she'll drink fresh milk.

What's the word *fresh* doing there? Many will interpret the
sentence to mean that without us she'll drink powdered or evap-
orated milk . . . and that isn't so bad, is it? (Should the sentence
be "Because of you she'll drink milk"? No, because *drink* isn't an
emotional kicker.)

The point: Consistent with the ancient maxim *Good writing
is lean*, genuine communicators should plow through the pile of
words, looking for—and mercilessly eliminating—Adjectival
Pitfalls.

"Turned Into" or "Became"?

"Turned into" is more immediate than "became." Sudden
change: "turned into"; gradual change: "became." We're describing a change. What's the difference between these two sentences?

- Dr. Jekyll turned into Mr. Hyde.
- Dr. Jekyll became Mr. Hyde.

Exactly! "Turned into" is more immediate; "became" is more
gradual. The difference between the two throwaways—as is true
of so many differences in these pages is lilliputian. Enough lilli-
putians can make an impact. What we've done, by deliberately
choosing one term over another, has been to take firm control of
the communication, leaving less interpretive latitude for our reader
or listener. We're *power* persuading.

Fig. 7.2

*This macho approach to advertising shows a he-man in a danger-
ous circumstance. The concept is strained, even without considering the gender of the benefit officer responsible for choosing
workers' compensation.*

STOP SMOKING

FREE 20 DAY TRIAL OFFER

MUSTOP provides the easy and economical way of stopping the desire to smoke immediately.

As part of a nationwide publicity campaign Bodywise Australia is offering Mustop in handy pocket sized spray dispensers on a 20 day free trial. You are the best judge of what works for you and we ask you merely to try Mustop free of charge for 20 days. You pay only if you decide to keep the product.

Simply spray "Mustop" from the unique dispenser into your mouth every morning.

You will taste a clean, fresh, peppermint flavour that has the effect of cleaning your breath. But when you light up your first cigarette of the day, "Mustop" goes to work immediately. Its formulated ingredients react with the nicotine to kill the desire to continue smoking. Nothing could be easier.

"Mustop" will continue to act in this way for up to five hours. Then, between four and five hours after the first application, simply repeat the dose and "Mustop" will act like "instant will-power" to help you stub out each cigarette you light up, after the first puff.

"Mustop" does not affect the taste of food or drink, in fact after a few minutes you will have forgotten you have used the spray.

It simply reactivates when your will weakens and continues to help you lose the desire to smoke until you are finally free from the harmful nicotine habit.

B.R. of Canterbury. *"I am now more than grateful that not only has your product suppressed my immediate desire for a cigarette but I am confident that by the time the month's treatment has elapsed that my system should be free of any craving for nicotine at all. I feel that I can fully endorse the claims of your product as a heavy smoker for some 20 years."*

MUSTOP is also available from selected pharmacies, supermarkets and most Woolworths stores in W.A. but not on a trial basis.

Bodywise
(division of Olner Pty Ltd Incorporated in NSW)
1st Fl. 535 Pittwater Rd, Brookvale NSW 2100. Telephone (02) 938 4488
Registered Victoria No. 22907

Send no money
satisfaction guaranteed
order today

MUSTOP FREE 20 DAY TRIAL AGREEMENT

Mail to: OLNER PTY LTD (inc. in NSW)
P.O. BOX 672, BROOKVALE N.S.W. 2100

I wish to try Mustop on a free 20 day trial and I agree that if I keep it for longer I will pay the retail price of $19.95.

NAME: Mrs/Ms/Miss/Mr _____

ADDRESS: _____

POSTCODE: _____ TELEPHONE: _____

SIGNED: _____

TTV1

Fig. 7.3

Macho or dainty? Macho, of course. Can you envision any sane copywriter heading this, "Do Stop Smoking"? The heading gains strength by having no exclamation point—it is both a promise and command.

The Difference Between "In Addition To" and "As Well As"

"As well as" is more assumptive than "In addition to," with a potentially negative connotation "In addition to" doesn't generate.

Example: "Am I interpreting your instructions correctly when I assume you want a stereo system [in addition to] [as well as] a projection video?"

"As well as" asks a second question . . . almost subliminally, but it's there. In statement as well as question, "as well as" includes a slight suggestion that enough exists without whatever follows.

Upgrading Terminology

Calling a booklet a "Special Report" increases the desire to acquire or buy. Exclusivity is one of the four great motivators. The others are: fear, greed, and guilt . . . plus an up-and-coming "possible"—need for approval. Fund-raisers have another "possible"—anger.

Macho or Dainty?

Is the trend toward unisex faltering? Indications ranging from low couture to magazine advertising suggest revival of masculine/feminine recognition . . . for *specific* circumstances, but not universally because of *The Dynamic Unisex Rule*:

- The more dynamic the message, the smaller the differential between masculine and feminine writing.

The "duosex" approach never totally died. It stood staunchly in the shadow of unisex flashy glitz, always available to the sophisticated marketer or to communicators aiming at the 50-plus age group.

Renewed interest in techniques of masculinizing or feminizing a message justifies a few tips for those acknowledging this throwback to earlier times.

For example, beginning the message with the word *Do* feminizes it. Test it for yourself. It works for every circumstance this writer can think of.

The hard-boiled imperative, "Make this a priority project" changes with the addition of *Do*: "Do make this a priority project." "Let me have your decision quickly" clarifies the sex of the sender when altered just a touch: "Do let me have your decision quickly."

The word *Just* can have a similar connotation, but only as a throwaway. The difference between "The book is jam-packed with useful information" and "The book is just jam-packed with useful information" is fractionally but definitely gender-related. "Just mail the coupon" has no gender.

Millions of words of copy, written to motivate millions of readers, listeners, and viewers, have resulted in this author compiling his personal list of terms which have motivational implications for one sex or the other.

A few words and phrases with decidedly feminine overtones:

adore	smashing
delightful	stylish
fashionable	thrilled, thrilling
heavenly	yes, but . . .
precious	

A few examples of the masculine/feminine differential:

masculine	feminine
cent	penny
crammed	brimming
because of	due to
I like to	I love to
loaded with	filled with
somebody	someone
underwear	undergarments
wrong	mistaken

Don't interpret *any* of this to suggest you descend into weakness or gushiness. *Mistaken* in no way has the guts of *wrong*. This analysis may help a male writer masquerade as he composes a letter. It may help a female writer avoid unconsciously defensive "toupée-on-the-chest" exposition.

Reciprocity calls for recognition of *Hey* and another word I just used, *guts,* as proprietary to beer-swillers.

Except for special circumstances, most communication is best when left sexless . . . but not emasculated.

A Suggestion? Or a Command?

The spoken word has an advantage over the written word: inflection.

Try saying, "I suggest you take advantage of this offer" three ways:

1. as a sincere suggestion;
2. as a veiled threat;
3. as a growled command.

You can do it. But in print, *suggest* doesn't have this versatility.

"I really do suggest you take advantage of this offer" adds a few teeth. "I think you should consider this offer very seriously" has so many teeth it can bite *you* instead of your potentially irritated target.

If you want the command-overtone without danger of reader-resentment, change the suggestion to a question: "Why not take advantage of this offer?"

The Rule of Acceptable Imperative underscores the value of insight into the relationship between message sender and message recipient:

- The degree of acceptable imperative depends on the message recipient's view of the relationship with the message sender.

Sincerity projected by the message sender affects reaction. So celebrity endorsements generate acceptance in ratio to the recipient's preconceived opinion of that celebrity—a caution flag for broadcast advertisers who may structure an entire imperative message around a celebrity.

Verisimilitude in Broadcast Testimonials

Testimonials have great verisimilitude *potential* in broadcast media. The introduction of a second voice into an announcement to deliver a testimonial works only if words and delivery both are credible. Less desirable but safer is the testimonial quoted by the announcer.

For television, showing a still photo of the person being quoted may be preferable to having that individual deliver the testimonial poorly on-camera.

The principal key to unlocking the door of skepticism barring viewer acceptance is credibility—and credibility is as much in the hands of the writer as it is in the hands of the celebrity. Do the words match the image? Does the delivery seem artificial because sentences are longer than one would expect from convivial conversation? Would a simple "I use it," "I drive it," or "I own one too" be a more convincing selling argument than pap-puffery?

These dimensions are the writer's call.

Chewable Bites

Spoken force-communication demands chewable bites. Short sentences, without parenthetical clauses, are easier to comprehend.

This suggests taking a look at compound sentences to determine the possibility of replacement with fast-comprehension shorter bursts. Consider too, for spoken force-communication, cutting into two pieces sentences starting with—

- An "As . . . as" phrase.
- Adverb-modified adjectives.
- ". . . ing" words.

Understand: Shortening the opening isn't a formula for brilliant broadcast copywriting. Rather, it's a formula for protecting you against target puzzlement or miscommunication.

Fig. 7.4

Volkswagen started a peculiar trend with the term "fahrvergneugen." Now Saudi Arabian Airlines says, "Ahlan Wasahlan." What does it mean? Confronting the prospective traveler with a term he or she probably doesn't understand accentuates the cultural gap the writer should be closing.

Why Imperatives Work in Broadcast Media

Imperatives work better in broadcast media than they do in print media. Easy proof: "Listen!" generates attention "Read!" never could.

Some examples of imperative immediacy:

- "Stop!"
- "Hold it right there!"
- "Wait!"
- "Come in!"
- "Come on!"
- "Go!"
- "Listen to this!"
- "Look at this!"
- "Watch this!"
- "Take a moment to . . ."
- "Grab your pencil and write this down."
- "Attention, please!"
- "Hurry!"

Most of these have exclamation points because spoken imperatives (in force-communication) should sound imperative.

The principle also works for non-command imperatives such as "Right now!" and "Hey!"

A Rare Opportunity

One of the delights of recognizing the power of throwaways is the opportunity—and it's a rare one in power communication—to use subtlety as a weapon. One admonition: Don't veil your message so heavily with throwaways you obscure the message.

Safety lies in avoiding subtlety. Once again, it's the writer's call: Do you want to be safe? Or do you want to risk scaling the communications mountain to its pinnacle and triumphantly plant your flag at the summit—knowing that you could slip and fall onto the jagged rocks below?

Chapter 8
The Power of Comparatives

I n any battle, the most potent weapon is also the most dangerous weapon. It can kill you instead of your target, especially
if you let half-trained troops load, aim, and fire it.

That's absolutely true of comparative advertising. Comparisons are an exquisite rapier. A skilled communications-swordsman
can run the competition through with a deft thrust; an inept word-
pusher, swinging comparatives with saber-like wildness, can kill
his own argument with inept swordplay.

In years past, many marketers feared comparisons. We were
likely to open Pandora's Box, giving free exposure to a rival (as
the television spots for Pepsi and Coke and many automobile and
computer manufacturers are doing now).

But today, with a more targeted and database-prompted
advertising ambience, we can assume the people at whom we aim
our messages have an existing competitive knowledge. So we're
able to apply **The Law of Comparative Advertising**:

> ■ If you're number 2 or smaller, attack a specific. If
> you're number 1, ridicule generic opposition; don't
> single out or respond to one target. Be certain your
> comparison caters to the reader's question: "What's
> in it for me?"

Ignoring that last caution means you're ignoring the reader.
The biggest mistake marketers make when they compare their
wares or services with a competitor's is forgetting (or worse,

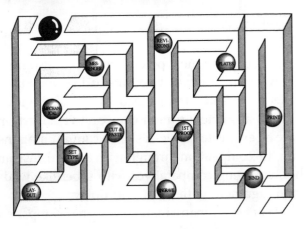

Now getting a document published can either be a maze...

Xerox puts it together a better way.
The Xerox DocuTech Production Publisher.

It used to be that to achieve high-quality, high-volume document production, business had one choice: the costly, time-consuming offset process.

But now you can get metal-plate, offset-like quality documents faster—with fewer steps than ever before.

With the new Xerox DocuTech Production Publisher. It's the first in a series of publishing products that put together three distinct technologies—digital scanning, laser imaging and xerography—into one simplified publishing solution.

Moreover, the Production Publisher uniquely fulfills your need for high quality, low cost and quick turnaround.

© 1991 XEROX CORPORATION. XEROX® and DOCUTECH are trademarks of the XEROX CORPORATION.

The DocuTech Production Publisher offers significant advantages over the traditional offset process by eliminating complicated pre-press operations.

It begins with the Production Publisher's built-in scanner that quickly captures text, line art and photos, and converts them to digital masters. The user interface then puts these digital masters at your command. No more time-consuming, tedious preparations. You can easily perform complicated cut-and-paste right at the user interface. Resizing, cropping, scaling and merging text with photos, are all easily executed. And with the image enhancement capabilities, copies of photographs, halftones and line art can actually surpass the original in quality.

Fig. 8.1
Well-constructed "Either . . . or . . ." comparisons are the height of the art in comparative advertising, this type of comparison perfectly suits the dominant company in a field.

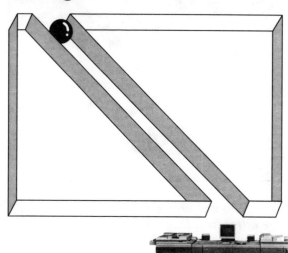
© 1992 The Dartnell Corporation

Fig. 8.2
By lumping all competitors into an "ordinary handwaxer" category, this ad trumpets, "We're better than they are." But the play on the words, "wide margin" (referring to a 3-inch roller compared with 1½-inch rollers), may be lost on many readers, and the buglike character astride the handwaxer has no significance.

ignoring) *why* they're advertising in the first place: to get some new business.

How about *positive* comparisons? We call these *touchstones*. The communicator who recognizes the types of touchstones and knows how to spawn one can make a silk purse out of a sow's-ear product or service.

Before getting to touchstones, a grittier communications challenge: competitive comparatives.

Four Competitive Comparative Techniques

Comparative advertising comes in more than one flavor. And, happily for the aggressive salesperson-in-print, one of those flavors is *always* available. If you want to write a comparative ad or mailer, you don't have to wait for results from a testing laboratory or user-survey; you just switch to another flavor.

Here are four:

1. We're better than they are. The knee-jerk reaction, when marketers discuss comparative advertising, is fishing around for a "We're better than they are" claim.

Okay . . . but add two additional elements, to qualify this first of the four most popular comparative approaches for congruence with the Law of Comparative Advertising:

1. I'll tell you why.
2. I'll tell you what it means to you.

You can see at once why this type of comparative, fleshed out, has such power: To mount the offensive, you have to load your rhetorical rifle with ammunition. You can't just wave it in the air or point it and shout, "Bang!" This means compiling a factual core of superiority, not only in mechanical or statistical terms but in a form translatable into reader benefit.

Plymouth automobiles originated the classic form of this comparative in the 1930s and 1940s, with a chart comparing the Plymouth with Ford and Chevrolet, not identified by name.

To this day, the comparison chart is an effective way of presenting a comparative argument. Its principal advantage is *clarity*. Its principal disadvantage is *inclusion of trivia*, resulting from a marketer's mad desire to empty the basket, including wood-shavings and apple-cores.

2. We're the greatest. This flat statement of total superiority stems as often from the ego of corporate management as it does from sound marketing principles.

That mildly pejorative comment is based on the observation of "crowing" which not only doesn't enhance image; it damages image, for two reasons. First, we naturally cheer for the underdog. Second, chest-thumping works only when the message recipient is either cowed or pre-convinced.

For heaven's sake, if you lean toward assuming an Olympian position, involve the reader. The reader doesn't care about your buildings or your multiplicity of awards or equipment not directly involved in making whatever the reader might buy. The reader doesn't accept your claim of "Service" or "Quality" or some other neutral marking-time word, without relevance.

So don't fall into the trap of describing what you have, when the reader keeps asking, "What will it do for *me*?"

Media—newspapers, magazines, broadcast stations, and cable channels—and computer hardware and software manufacturers are the most prone to use this second type of comparative. I'm looking at an ad for Nickelodeon. The heading:

WE STOMP THE COMPETITION.
Kids watch Nickelodeon more than the kids'
programming on the three broadcast networks
combined.

Illustration is a cartoon dinosaur, labeled "30.3% NICKELODEON," stomping the logos of NBC ("6.2%"), CBS ("6.7%"), and ABC ("8.1%"). Imagine how flat the ad would be without backup evidence.

3. We were marvelous before, and now we're even better. (Note the word "and" instead of "but." See chapter 3 for the reason.)

The advantage of this comparative variation is obvious: You don't need an external target. The comparison is *internal*.

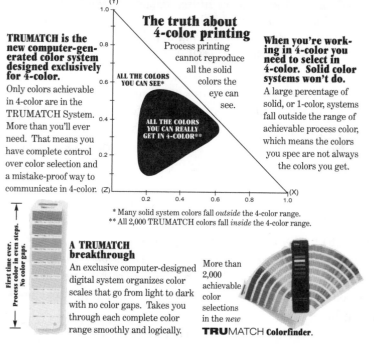

Why the solid color system you're using now isn't best for 4-color jobs.

Many solid colors aren't matchable in 4-color. TRUMATCH gives you over 2,000 colors–all of them on target.

TRUMATCH is the new computer-generated color system designed exclusively for 4-color.

Only colors achievable in 4-color are in the TRUMATCH System. More than you'll ever need. That means you have complete control over color selection and a mistake-proof way to communicate in 4-color.

The truth about 4-color printing

Process printing cannot reproduce all the solid colors the eye can see.

ALL THE COLORS YOU CAN SEE*

ALL THE COLORS YOU CAN REALLY GET IN 4-COLOR**

When you're working in 4-color you need to select in 4-color. Solid color systems won't do.

A large percentage of solid, or 1-color, systems fall outside the range of achievable process color, which means the colors you spec are not always the colors you get.

* Many solid system colors fall *outside* the 4-color range.
** All 2,000 TRUMATCH colors fall *inside* the 4-color range.

First time ever. Process color in even steps. No color gaps.

A TRUMATCH breakthrough

An exclusive computer-designed digital system organizes color scales that go from light to dark with no color gaps. Takes you through each complete color range smoothly and logically.

More than 2,000 achievable color selections in the *new* **TRU**MATCH **Colorfinder.**

Fig. 8.3

A "why" headline is provocative because the reader anticipates getting inside information. In this case, the writer couples "why" with a negative and a claim of superiority. It's a difficult approach and only partly successful because of the unexplained (and unnecessary?) X-Y-Z chart and because of the undefined "many" competitors.

Fig. 8.4
"We are the greatest" comes in two flavors: certified and uncertified. This car dealer's copy says, "Our parts dept. is ranked #1 in the United States!" By whom—the manufacturer? How much more powerful would this ad have been had it said so?

This is the way to flaunt awards and testimonials. It's especially useful when customers who used to buy from another source give you permission to quote them on switching to you.

Should you pitch new buildings and equipment? Oh, if you have to . . . but I, for one, respond with profound apathy to such hogwash as "We've Moved to 333 W. 33rd Street, in Order to Serve You Better." Whenever we read this kind of trivial bomblet, we wonder whether the writer mightn't have worked just a little harder to find a reader-involving hook.

4. Made to Sell for X-Dollars . . . Yours for Y-Dollars. Here we have an unassailable comparative because this one, like number 3, is self-generated. The comparison is founded on solid air—what might have been.

A good writer can make a beanstalk out of this seed, because the very word *Yours* is reader-involving. If we do accept the catechism that the reader doesn't care what it is, but rather what's the comparative benefit for him/her, this becomes a useful device.

The fourth comparative is a pleasure to have at hand when you don't have other grenades to throw. And the comparison doesn't have to be dollars. It can be amount. It can be speed. It can be an upgrade. It can be a bonus item. All qualify if the writer *compares* them with what might have been, what others have paid or will pay, or what will be after the expiration date.

A Few Automatic Helpers

One way to avoid the trap of describing what you have, leaving the stranded reader to ask, "What will it do for *me*?" is to start the message with reader-involving catch-all phrases such as "At last!"

"At last!" pushes a message into a reader-involving direction. "You've never seen . . ." or "You've been waiting for . . ." are similar but less dynamic natural channels.

If you begin your sales argument with "Which would you rather [have, do, be]?"—or "Five years from now, will you . . ." —you've directed your communication into an automatic self-serving, reader-involving comparative.

What the serious power communicator might do, when the moon is full, is begin a compilation of phrases such as these. A big benefit: You'll never be stuck for an effective opener.

The "Selective Spokesperson" as Typical Testimonial

To imply universal acceptance in the absence of multiple testimonials, create an impression of bulk acceptance or preference by naming a "selective spokesperson." **Example:**

> *One knowledgeable distributor summarized his reaction this way: "It's beyond argument. I've never seen, let alone sold, one this good."*

Kids will be kids. Unless it takes you 42 years to reach them.

There's been lots of talk about the #1 kids channel, and how the networks are being trampled.

Who's kidding who?

NBC draws five times more kids Saturday morning than Nickelodeon does. And primetime hits draw millions more.

Truth is, at their current rate of growth, it'll take Nickelodeon 42 years to reach the same numbers that we do Saturday morning. Last year, in fact, their ratings were flat.

In the meantime, our kids will have grown up, spent big bucks on toys, snacks and sneakers, got married and begun their own families.

It's simple. Buy the network that delivers kids while they're still kids. Not when they've got kids of their own.

NBC. STILL THE PLACE TO BE.

Source: Kids 2-11 NHI Fourth quarter 1988, 1989, 1990 Saturday 8AM-1PM; NTI: 4th quarter 1990 Saturday 8AM-12 Noon.

Fig. 8.5

Would this ad have been more effective with a directly comparative headline? Maybe. In an advertising trade magazine, a wryly-made point can be lost by depending on the reader to reach the comparison in the third paragraph. Those who do read that far will recognize unassailable superiority, projected with good-nature and class.

Since Nickelodeon became the #1 network for kids our ad sales have gone sky high.

Our five biggest advertisers increased spending 62% this year. The same five advertisers only increased their spending on the broadcast networks' kids' shows by 39%.

It is a time of tight budgets. It is also a time when television advertisers who want to reach children have more places to choose from than ever before.

That's why we're particularly proud that in 1990, Nickelodeon's five best customers—including some of the biggest names in toys, cereals, candy and snacks—chose to increase their spending with us by 62%.

What is it about Nickelodeon that appeals to these giants of the industry? It isn't the awards we won this year, or our new studio in Orlando.

It's the fact that children watch Nickelodeon more than the kids' programming on the three broadcast networks *combined*. Rock-solid numbers—that's what sent our ad sales soaring. And we look forward to even higher times ahead.

62%

39%
ABC NBC CBS

NICKELODEON

The #1 network for kids.

NICKELODEON

Fig. 8.6

Nickelodeon presents statistical comparative evidence in an unconventional way. Nickelodeon can't claim audience-dominance over the three major networks, so it selects a favorable statistic: increase in advertiser spending.

The selective spokesman, by his very role as spokesman, seems to represent others.

Arguably and *Perhaps*

The words *arguably* and *perhaps* can give authority to a statement which has no other foundation. **Examples:**

- This area is arguably one of the fastest-growing in the nation.
- "This word processing program is perhaps the most user-friendly in the history of personal computing."

Can you see the benefit? We haven't tampered with fact. We've used two *opinion*-founded words the reader will interpret favorably. Keep *arguably* and *perhaps* in your back pocket as emergency tourniquets when your sales argument staggers for want of foundation.

Warning: Don't use *perhaps* when you mean *maybe*, except when you want a touch of formality.

Apparent Validation

When you have an unprovable claim, these three openings *appear to be* validation: "We believe . . ."; "We've come to feel . . ."; "In our [considered] opinion . . ."

Generic Damning of the Competition

Since we're discussing the power (and it's a *mighty* power) of assuming a superior posture relative to competitors, here's

The new look of power just got more powerful.

Fig. 8.7

One of the four most recognizable techniques for declaring superiority is "We were marvelous before, and now we're even better." This Texas Instruments ad's heading lacks novelty but qualified absolutely for this approach. The first word of body copy, "Finally," also adds to the claim of superiority.

Fig. 8.8

A sensible rule for business-to-business advertisers: User testimonials have greater credibility than endorsement by celebrities unrelated to what you're selling. Here, however, the testimonial is toothless because "everything we need" can conjure up endless jokes about this accounting software.

another way to achieve the image of comparative superiority when a direct product comparison is impractical.

Generic damning of the competition achieves the image of superiority. The three key words are "Unlike others which. . . ." For example: "Unlike other models which vibrate as they engrave on metal, this one has a rotating point that completely eliminates vibration."

An ethical corporate attitude might object, "But you're suggesting *all* others vibrate." "Exactly," argues a cold-blooded copywriter. "We're talking salesmanship here, not ethics. Power copywriting includes, as a lovely by-product, the ability to change the reader's interpretation *without changing the facts*. So ethics aren't in question, because we *haven't* changed the facts."

The copywriter's justification—salesmanship—is unassailable from the viewpoint of hard-boiled business tactics. A corporate attitude so hyper-sensitive that it strangles salesmanship can result in a receiver's auction of your assets. But how pyrrhic and ethically skinny a victory it is . . . and how sad a moment for the whole universe of power copywriting, when the writer has to admit: "I didn't really sell this to the reader. I outwitted him."

"Double Damning"

"Double damning" tints criticism with ridicule.

Double damning is a rhetorical trick built into the genes of debate teams and politicians. The procedure is simple enough. In fact, we can mechanize it: To double-damn, first we deny finding fault. Then we name a flaw with which we aren't finding fault. Then we name a second flaw with which we *are* finding fault. The reader or listener recognizes both faults, but we, in a singular act of statesmanship, have denied criticizing the first.

Out of a thousand FSI's, 997 miss the target. So much for "Cost Per Thousand."

A low cost per thousand can be highly expensive. Because out of 1,000 FSI's, only 3 are redeemed by your real target: users of competitive brands. The rest go astray. In fact, 975 never get redeemed at all.

In contrast, Checkout Coupon® only issues coupons to your target. Using scanner data right at the checkstand, we generate a coupon when a shopper buys a product you've specified in advance. Such as a competitive brand.

So, instead of cost per thousand, you can judge us by how well we perform against specific objectives, set up ahead of time.

Not only do we eliminate waste. Once we've captured new customers for you, we help you keep them. With ongoing programs that issue more incentives, reinforcing the change in purchase behavior.

The Checkout Coupon system reaches over 30 million households each week. And we never miss. Call Catalina Marketing, 721 East Ball Road, Suite 200, Anaheim, CA 92805. (800) 955-9770

CHECKOUT COUPON▌▌▌▌▌®

Fig. 8.9
Suppliers to advertisers are fiercely competitive. This communication, in an advertising publication, depends on competitive ridicule. Some confusion attends this exposition because the illustration, which intends to show a woman crumpling an FSI, instead looks like a meteorite. But the comparison is absolute, specific, and hard-boiled.

I'm not criticizing the lack of grammar; I'm criticizing the lack of good judgment.

By the very reference, the writer ridicules grammar.

Superior, **not** *Different*

Effective comparatives recognize *The Comparative Superiority of Superiors Rule*:

- When comparing yours with theirs, use words suggesting superiority rather than difference.

This Rule calls into question the word *different* itself.

Copy for computer software has this selling argument:

It's as big a difference from other methods of data retrieval as a 747 airplane is from the Wright Brothers' first model.

Not bad. Superiority is both implicit and explicit. The thinness here isn't the comparison between the 747 and the Wright Brothers; no, it's suggesting they're *different* from each other instead of suggesting ours is better than theirs.

A tiny change gives us:

It's as big an advance over other methods of data retrieval as a 747 airplane is over the Wright Brothers' first model.

We've skewed the comparison to favor us. That's what our job is supposed to be, isn't it?

Adjectival Damning of the Competition

If what you have is extraordinary, what the competition has is . . . ordinary, of course.

Calling anything "ordinary" turns it negative; in a comparison, yours becomes positive by default.

Ordinary is obvious, but what about *synonyms* of "ordinary"?

In descending order, depending on how negative you want the competition to appear to be: "This light green color is easier on the eyes than [regular] [standard] [ordinary] white paper." If you really want to slam, call the competition "old-fashioned."

Does the Comparison Make Sense?

A major international airline, extolling its virtues in broadcast ads, referred to "A passion that comes not from the head but from the heart."

Now, what the devil does that mean?

To the television viewer or the radio listener, nothing much. The comparison is a mismatch. Passion is implicitly emotional. So how can "passion from the head" exist?

When a would-be communicator decides to play with words as though they were Silly Putty instead of using them like Lego blocks, artifice replaces communication.

When You Want to Compare But Have No Basis for Comparison

For an unprovable claim, the doubled comparative adjective solves a persuasion problem the single comparative adjective can't solve.

Example: "More and more . . ." and "Less and less . . ." are better than "More" or "Less."

More or *Less* implicitly demand a *than*—and "More than . . ." or "Less than . . ." in turn demand a specific comparison.

"More and more" doesn't have this problem. **Example:**

More dentists endorse this new non-abrasive tooth-whitener.

The message is incomplete, and an incomplete message is implicitly weak: *More,* unexplained, draws no comparison.

That's the value of the second *More.* Comparison is automatic, eliminating the specificity we'd *have* to have if we added the mandatory "than . . ."

More and more dentists endorse this new non-abrasive tooth-whitener.

More and *Less* are only two of the comparative adjectives which fit this mold. A few others: Fewer; bigger; greater; cheaper; stronger; and almost any adjective ending in "er."

How About a Little Hyperbole?

Hyperbole implicitly suggests superiority. But when the person at whom you aim the message *recognizes* your statement as hyperbole, you have a problem: Your best buyer now disbelieves the hyperbole *and,* possibly, the tangible product benefits behind the claim.

So we have *The Rule of Hyperbole Diminution*:

- The better your prospect matches what you have to sell, the farther you'll drive him off by useless hyperbole.

Exaggerated statements sometimes work, especially if the reader doesn't bother to penetrate the nonlogic. Exaggeration has to be handled like a truckload of filled septic tanks when you're advertising to individuals who, because they have the background to evaluate your pitch, can use your overstatement as the excuse to ignore—or worse, reject—the whole message.

An example is one unnecessary and out-of-key word in this sales letter:

[NAME OF COMPANY]'s exclusive data base contains the names of all sizes and types of direct marketing industry firms and the people at those firms responsible for the primary buying decisions.

Over the past two years, we have invested almost a million dollars to research and update this comprehensive list. You now can rent this priceless information for just pennies per name.

Of course you spotted the word: *priceless*. Calling a list of direct marketing executives priceless flatters the industry but hardly represents the fact; suggesting we can rent each priceless name for pennies weakens the validity of the whole offer. In two minutes any of us can think of two dozen parallel words we'd have accepted without question.

Proprietary Exclusion

An unattackable position of superiority where no actual superiority exists? That's the benefit of *proprietary exclusion.*

Proprietary exclusion is absolute but without references to competitors . . . so to counterattack, competitors either have to make a weak claim of equivalence—"Me, too"—or fight a shadow.

Proprietary exclusion usually claims a *geographic area* rather than a product differential. This gives the claim a unique absoluteness.

Examples:

- America's Sweetheart
- Pittsburgh's low-cost insurance company
- The Valley's Own Walnut Headquarters

Proprietary exclusion makes questionable claims of superiority unnecessary ("Pittsburgh's best insurance company" has no punch whatever).

Superlative Might Not Be Comparative

Superlatives have an obvious function and a subtle function.

The obvious function is the statement of supremacy: "I am the greatest"; "Best car on the road."

The subtle function can be codified into a rule, ***The Superlative Identification Rule***:

- The superlative can help identify.

Unexplained, this concept can only cause wrinkled brows. In practice, it can help clarify a communications point to our always-skeptical, usually-half-comprehending readers. Compare these two descriptions:

Fig. 8.10
Phrased as a question, this claim of superiority gains strength because the answer—immediate and prominent—may not be what many readers anticipate. When proposing a "surprise" declaration of supremacy, questions are effective devices.

You can carry it in a tiny purse.

or—

You can carry it in the tiniest purse.

The second version helps identify the size. By tying it to an extreme instead of a generic, we enhance reader confidence. An example in the other direction:

One spraying covers even a big room.

or—

One spraying covers even the biggest room.

Analyzing a claim of size or strength or longevity or beauty or pleasure, the communicator asks, "Have I convinced skeptical readers? And have I convinced the most skeptical readers?" In those two questions you see the extra octane a shift to the superlative brings to this type of narrative or description.

Parity Advertising

In the absence of superiority, equivalence is a useful sales argument: "No bank gives you higher interest" or "Nobody—but nobody—undersells Brown's" *seems to be* a statement of superiority. Actually, the statement is one of equivalence.

One of the great clichés of advertising, "If you can find a better [whatever], buy it," seems to be a statement of superiority but actually is no claim at all.

This is *parity* advertising. Its value comes from being the first of a group of indistinguishable competitors to seize and use it. (Note: Chapter 6 describes *negative* parity.)

Touchstones: High Art in Communication

Touchstones are such gloriously simple and available direct marketing communication weapons it's surprising they aren't used more often.

It's more disappointing than surprising when a sales argument that easily could swing its thrust to a touchstone ignores this happy crutch and veers instead into overblown bombast. The writer or speaker hasn't taken advantage of the difference between quasi-logic and admitted pleading, between quasi-power and admitted weakness, between quasi-guilt generation and bluster.

Yes, each difference carries a *quasi*-qualification—because touchstone-based wording isn't really logical or powerful or guilt-generating. Why? Touchstones are an artifice, and any artificial structure is by its very nature *quasi*.

Touchstones Defined

What, exactly, is a touchstone?

A touchstone is a recognizable, approved episode used to anchor an otherwise unrecognizable, unapproved episode. In two words: It's coattail-riding.

A letter begins:

Dear Executive:
475 of the Fortune 500 companies are now US SPRINT
customers . . .

The coattails this company rides are contemporaneous; historical coattails are equally valuable, especially since they don't have to relate to the marketer using them. Some examples follow.

Collectibles regularly use touchstones as evidence of their potential worth. Quite right, too: After all, how else can a vendor suggest potential value in advance of historical evidence? So a classic collectible mail order pitch begins:

Dear Friend:

Suppose that twenty-five years ago the Chairman of IBM had offered you stock in his company, and guaranteed to buy it back any time during the first year for the full price you paid . . .

Of course that didn't happen. Most opportunities don't come with guarantees. But I'm about to describe a collector's plate that does.

"Pao-chai," the first plate in the new Beauties of the Red Mansion series . . .

Get the pitch? This company might have *started* its letter with the standard "You don't take any risk" approach we all know so well and use so heavily. Instead, it grabs the coattails of IBM in a "What if?" approach, giving us a *touchstone* we recognize. IBM is the touchstone, and the intention—cynical or not—is to transfer our unquestioned acceptance of the touchstone to an unquestioned acceptance of the coattail reference.

Fig. 8.11
Coattail-riding isn't admirable, but consider the ambience: This is a table-tent designed for bars and taverns. The advertiser wants two reactions: 1. an "America's finest" tie between branches of the armed services and the beer; 2. a subliminal imprint which might result in asking the bartender for a Bud (instead of just a beer).

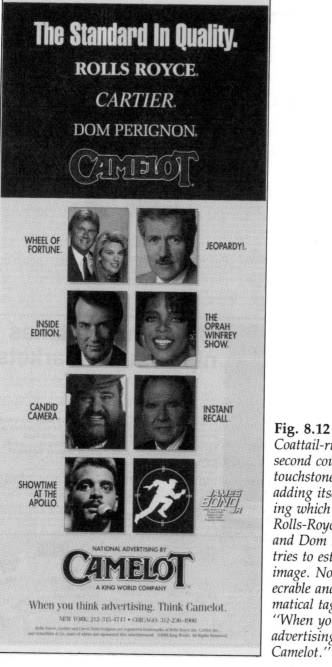

Fig. 8.12
Coattail-ridings are second cousins to touchstones. Camelot, adding itself to a listing which includes Rolls-Royce, Cartier, and Dom Perignon, tries to establish an image. Notice the execrable and ungrammatical tag line: "When you think advertising. Think Camelot."

Simplest of All: Dollar and Historical Touchstones

Even more common is the Dollar Touchstone. Because this and the Historical Touchstone are the simplest, most primitive of all touchstones, the Dollar Touchstone is readily available.

This opening typifies the Dollar Touchstone:

Dear Collector:

Today I am delighted to announce an event which is sure to produce immediate and intense interest among knowledgeable collectors. This special premiere marks the first-ever limited-edition plate by famed naturalist art master Paul J. Sweany.

*As you may know, **first-ever** plates from important and well-known artists have shown strong and consistent price appreciation on today's secondary market. For example, the 1976 "Los Ninos," first plate by the famous Southwest artist Ted DeGrazia, has soared from an original price of $35.00 to a current level of $1800 for an increase of 5043%!*

Like "Los Ninos," Sweany's new "Spicebush Swallowtail" plate exhibits a fresh and distinctive art style . . .

(Even better for an uncertain communicator, the Dollar Touchstone doesn't require a direct connection. It parallels this sales argument: "Remember how people thought Edison was addled and Einstein was retarded? Well, my kid . . .")

See how easy? See how much more logical it *seems* than the bare introduction of an art product by a little-known artist?

Here's a variation on the same theme. Two quick questions:

1. Who is James Bond?
2. Who was Sidney Reilly?

The questions aren't quite fair, not only because even inhabitants of the planet Mars know James Bond but also because, in context, a handful might know Sidney Reilly. But what a perfect opportunity for a touchstone! So a book catalog doesn't feature the titles of three books about Reilly (the best-known book: *Reilly: Ace of Spies*). Instead, the heading is:

THE REAL JAMES BOND

History is grist for the touchstone mill. Think how many mailings you've opened over the years, finding a sales argument such as, "Don't you wish you could have bought Miami Beach land in the 1920s, when it was selling for $10 an acre?" or, "You may not have been able to cash in on the last precious metals surge, when the price of gold shot up from $100 to $800 an ounce. Yours may not have been one of the vast fortunes made then. But now . . ."

A mailing offering "the personally-signed memoirs of all four of America's living past Presidents" doesn't let the questionable value of these men's signatures totter unsupported. Instead, it gold-sprays their names with unassailable touchstones:

> . . . *Think about the significance. Just imagine if today you owned the personally-signed memoirs of Jefferson, Lincoln, Truman or Eisenhower.*

Logical? Of course not. More powerful than a nontouchstone pitch for undistinguished "coffee table" books? You bet. If you'd been hired to write this message, would you have thought of it?

"As . . . As" Paralleling Touchstones

- As fast as . . .
- As beautiful as . . .
- As big as . . .
- As happy as . . .

Some of these parallels are so common they're clichés: "He's as happy as a clam"; "It's as big as a house"; "The team is as hot as a firecracker."

The "as . . . as" paralleling touchstones are easy to assemble. All you have to do is think of the best item or circumstance representative of your intention; then name it.

Suppose you manufacture a steno chair. You write, "As comfortable as . . ." and then reconnoiter. What's comfortable? A cloud? A feather-bed? That's the other half of the "as" equation.

The benefit of the "as . . . as" paralleling touchstone is that it requires *no* research, *no* proof, *no* validation. It's poetry rather than fact, which means you don't even have to get up from your comfortable-as-a-soft-massage steno chair to find usable ammunition.

A negative aspect: "As . . . as" isn't as dynamic as other paralleling touchstones. For example, "You'll have access to data as fast as brokers get that same data" doesn't have the impact a non-"as" version has: "You'll have access to data the same instant brokers get that same data."

The Two Touchstone Rules

Effective touchstones conform to two Touchstone Rules. *The First Touchstone Rule*:

■ To be effective, the touchstone should be recognized by the reader.

So we can't begin a mailing to random Spencer Gifts buyers with, "What if you could have heard Schopenhauer or Maimonides discourse on the implied benevolence of mankind?"

Nor can we use the rock group 2 Live Crew as a touchstone in our mailing to members of the Brahms Society.

What we *can* do is educate and touch in the same description, as this catalog copy does:

SET OF IMARI SERVING BOWLS, lavishly decorated in the 200-year-old tradition of Japanese Imari porcelain . . .

Deceptively simple. We don't alienate those who already know what Imari is, and we bring into orbit those who don't.

And for impact we add *The Second Touchstone Rule*:

■ If the touchstone is actually within the reader's experiential background, impact and credibility increase in direct ratio to emotional acceptance of the memory.

This Second Rule isn't as basic, so it isn't as easy to implement. But even though it's not for beginners, neither is it abstruse. Two key nouns describe it: *nostalgia* or *greed*. (If you can find a *nostalgic greed* touchstone, you can't miss!)

Fig. 8.13

This advertisement uses the touchstone technique to emphasize the year that the company was founded. An effective ad? No. The writer of this ad leaves interpretation to the reader, which is an especially difficult job because the illustration relates only to the touchstone.

So this letter opening is an exemplar of the Second Touchstone Rule, regardless of imperfections in the copy itself:

Dear Friend:

Can you remember what it was like?

> *The movie theater darkened, the curtains parted, and there, up on the screen, marvelous children's stories unfolded in a wondrous combination of color, art, movement, and sound that can only be described as pure magic.*

> *No matter how old we were when we saw our first Disney animated film . . .*

Sure, magic bleeds out of the message almost as fast as the nostalgia touchstone pumps it in: A too-long early sentence uses colorless phrases and words such as "marvelous children's stories" and "wondrous combination" and the damaging "animated film." But even these can't mortally wound the grabber opening, "Can you remember what it was like?"

How to Find a Touchstone

To generate a touchstone, the communicator asks just one question: What object or event of greatest significance to the reader has an emotional relationship with what I'm selling?

Get that qualifier. It *isn't* just the object or event of greatest significance. It's the object or event of greatest significance *to the reader*. Following the First Touchstone Rule prevents the writer from lapsing into a private world—or, worse, from showing off at the expense of reader rapport.

The writer who rushes from project to project could profit from compiling a generic file of Noteworthy Touchstones.

Five Easy Pieces

Here, as a contribution to smooth those days when the muse isn't with you, are five royalty-free touchstone openings. (Don't overestimate the gift. Nobody can claim these will lead to brilliant communication; we can claim only that they're more reader-motivating than wild dependence on unproved superlatives.)

1. "Maybe you couldn't have [been with WHOEVER] [done WHATEVER] accompanied [WHOMEVER] . . . but you can . . ."
2. "Move over, [NAME or WHATEVER] . . ." or "Do you want to join [WHOEVER]?"
3. "When [NAME] began [WHATEVER] he/she couldn't have anticipated . . ."
4. "In the tradition of . . ." or "Remember when . . ."
5. "What if . . ."

Careful! The [WHATEVER/WHOEVER] reference shouldn't betray your motive. Pre-tying the link dilutes the purity of the touchstone.

Example: We're selling recordings. Our touchstone might be, "Maybe you couldn't have been in the concert hall the night Shostakovich conducted his fifth symphony. But . . ."

Example: We're selling insurance. Our touchstone might be, "You may not have the nerve or the build to match the chorus-girl who insured her legs for $1 million, but . . ."

Example: We're selling jewelry. Our touchstone might be, "Have you ever, on the way home from a dinner party, wondered with just a touch of envy, 'I wonder how she could afford to buy that huge diamond ring . . .'"

Example: We're selling travel. Our touchstone might be, "At the turn of the century a few of the very rich planned an incredible 'Journey of a Lifetime' . . ."

Example: We're selling cookbooks. Our touchstone might be, "Remember when you were a child and went to Grandma's house? She always baked a special pie for you, and nobody could match her dinner recipes. In this world of prepackaged foods you might have thought those wonderful old-time recipes were gone forever . . ."

Example: We're selling a communications technique. Our touchstone might be, "Remember all the touchstones you've read about today, and how simple they are to construct even when you don't have a creative idea in your head? Well, now it's your turn . . . ."

Chapter 9
This, That, and the Other Thing

The power communicator can prove, easily enough, that his or her craft is as much discipline as it is instinct. This proof lies in the *conscious* decision to use (or eliminate) specific words.

For example: Had the first sentence of this chapter read, "The power communicator can prove, easily enough, his or her craft is as much discipline as it is instinct," had the second sentence read; "That proof lies in the *conscious* decision to use (or eliminate) specific words;" or had either sentence begun, "It is easy enough to demonstrate that . . .;" the message would have been similar but not identical.

Why insert or remove the word *that*? Why use *This* instead of *that*, or vice-versa? What's wrong with starting a message with the word *It*?

Let's take a look.

That-Bashing Revisited

That-bashing may have gone too far.

This author joined the *that*-bashers club some years ago when Frank Schultz, the now-retired genius who superimposed Texas Royal Ruby Red Grapefruit onto the consciousness of two generations of fruit-by-mail buyers, plowed through a piece of copy, exorcising every *that*.

He was right, of course, in almost every instance, and the author became his *that*-bashing disciple. But overzealous *that*-bashing can violate the Clarity Commandment, and in a head-to-head slugfest The Clarity Commandment had better win every time, or your keyboard is firing blanks.

The Clarity Commandment revisited:

- In force-communication, clarity is paramount. Don't let any other component of the communications mix interfere with it.

Sure, Joyce Kilmer's poem wouldn't scan without *that*—I think I shall never see / A poem as lovely as a tree.

That isn't what this means; nor does it mean use of the word as a pronoun, as it was used to start this sentence. We're talking clarity here. Make your own choice: Is this next sentence clearer with or without *that*?

Take a look at an example that speaks for itself:

Okay, the text just did. What sense does the sentence make without "that"?

Another:

I've come to think [that] the use of that *depends on clarity.*

One more:

I doubt [that] you can read this sentence straight through.

Without *that*, you can't, because "I doubt you" makes sense on its own.

Oh, yes, let's keep the *that*-swatter at hand. But think of "that" the way you think of cholesterol: We have good "thats" and we have bad "thats." At least, *that's* what this writer thinks.

Fig. 9.1

"That-bashers" take heart—your mill may never run out of grist. This text has two quick and surplus "thats" in consecutive sentences. Add the nondescript noun "needs," an "As . . ." paragraph opening, and "service" as the final word, and you have a message with less impact than it might have had. Running type over a dark background certainly doesn't help.

Receive—a Passive Word

How many letters have you written, using the word *receive* or *received* in the first sentence? Stop it, please.

"Received" is passive. A victim *receives* a fatal wound; a criminal *receives* a sentence. The recipient has no active part in the process.

So "When you get your first issue and free diskette" has considerably greater reader involvement than "When you receive your first issue and free diskette," which puts the seller in a position of dominance. A prospective subscriber feels uncomfortable in a secondary position . . . probably without quite knowing why.

"When you get your first catalog . . ." makes the reader a

partner in a way "When you receive your first catalog . . ." can't.

Get and *Got* are more than synonyms for *receive* and *received*. They have value as replacements for *become/became*. Because of their consistent mildly possessive overtone, the words suggest or show responsibility:

- "She got lost on the way here" is more her fault than . . .
- "She became lost on the way here."
- "His work got better" is more the result of his dynamic action than "His work was better" or "His work became better."

Get makes some writers itchy because it's a guttural word. That quality is why good salespeople use it so much.

It: **Don't Start with It**

It is one of the weakest words to open a selling argument.

Just look through anything you've written, looking for openings such as "It is" or "It was" or "It doesn't." We've known the weakness of *It* since Bulwer-Lytton's famous/infamous "It was a dark and stormy night." With one exception, we always can generate a stronger opening than the word *It*.

A few examples of *It* and ways to achieve *It*-opening avoidance:

1. Instead of, "It doesn't take a crystal ball to tell you interactive television is a powerful marketing force," write or say, "You don't need a crystal ball to tell you interactive television is a powerful marketing force." Can anyone argue in favor of the *It* version?

2. Instead of, "It is my privilege to invite you to become a member of a unique club," write or say, "I'm [or I am] privileged to invite you to become a member of a unique club."

3. Instead of, "It will take a few minutes of your time to read my letter and to fill out the membership application," write or say, "Take a few minutes to read my letter and to fill out the membership application." (The revision dropped the additional weakener-contributor "of your time" as an additional benefit. Without "It will take," the phrase is redundant.)

Now, what's the exception?

"It was," *followed by a predicate nominative*, adds historicity to fact:

Instead of "Harald Bing, head of the Danish porcelain house Bing and Grøndahl, in 1895 issued the first limited edition plate," your copy gains historical drama by *preceding the fact* with *It*: "It was Harald Bing, head of the Danish porcelain house Bing and Grøndahl, who in 1895 issued the first limited edition plate."

Why does this work? "It was," in this use, tells us a revelation is coming up. Yes, the gap is only a second or so, but what the heck—every little bit helps.

("It was a dark and stormy night" *doesn't* qualify, because even though "a dark and stormy night" is a predicate nominative, the phrase provides neither revelation nor historicity.)

Nouns for Clarity, Pronouns for Marking Time

The earlier you introduce a noun, the clearer the message becomes.

Check your copy for *concept-introduction*. If you refer to *it* or *them* before actually naming whatever it is, you're sapping clarity out of your message.

An example:

*Only when we're convinced it will be a joyful project
for every reader do we publish a pattern.*

"It" precedes what it *is*—"pattern." So if we rewrite for lucidity we change the sentence to:

*Only when we're convinced a pattern will be a joyful
project for every reader do we publish it.*

This procedure has an ancillary benefit: It also helps block a lapse into nondescript poetry. (Note the sequence of the previous sentence: "Procedure" precedes "It.")

Nouns Versus Verbs and Adjectives

When making word choices, consider the difference in power between nouns and their verb or adjective parallels. The same word roots transmit messages the sender may think are identical but whose strength differs in the target-reaction they generate.

Nouns are identifiers, implicitly more powerful than verbs or adjectives. Compare . . .

(Verb) I drink.

or—

(Noun) I'm a drinker.

(Adjective) I'm cynical.

or—

(Noun) I'm a cynic.

The difference in power stems from the very nature of nouns. Nouns are names while verbs are action-describers and adjectives are attributes.

A name is absolute; an attribute may be one of many. So "He's a moron" *names* him; "moron" is the only identifier. "He's moronic" singles out a characteristic but doesn't implictly exclude other characteristics. So we see **The Rule of Noun Dominance**:

■ Nouns overpower adjectives.

We communicators are adjective-happy. We inject an offbeat adjective such as *fiery* or *sumptuous* and our day is made. It shouldn't be. Instead, we should grope around for ways to replace adjectives with nouns.

An example: "We have an unequalled expert staff" is weaker than "We have an unequalled staff of experts."

Look for words which are both nouns and adjectives. Sometimes you can hyphenate to turn them into a single power-word. Example: "Power-word."

The First Word Sets the Tone

In titles, the first word has greatest influence on reader or listener reaction. If that word is a noun, it has greater consequence than if it were an adjective, because of The Rule of Noun Dominance.

It's not
a pool.
It's our sea.

Crystal clear waters, outrageously beautiful flowers, lush tropical greenery—they're all part of a vacation in the United States Virgin Islands. Just think—all this natural beauty surrounds luxurious resorts, historic towns, world-class dining and world-class shopping. See your travel agent.

St.Croix St.John St.Thomas
The American paradise. United States Virgin Islands
© 1990 USVI Division of Tourism: Atlanta, Chicago, LA, Miami, NYC & D.C.

Fig. 9.2

"It" is one of the weakest words to open a selling argument. Coupled with "not," weakness is compounded—unless the writer's intent is to draw a wry parallel (as it is here). Still, a stronger first word would have meant a more dynamic message.

So to make a job title more consequential, it's Director of Marketing, not Marketing Director. It's Vice President of Engineering, not Engineering Vice President. The Manager of Purchasing seems to outrank the Purchasing Manager.

The principle works for nonpersonal references: Our magazine is Number One in the world of photography, not Number One in the photographic world.

Consider this point before the next reprint of your business cards.

Active or Passive Voice?

We all know the superiority of active voice over passive. But, all generalizations being false, exceptions exist.

1. Active voice usually is superior to passive voice, but passive is valuable for shifting responsibility-intention.
2. Active voice usually is superior to passive voice, but passive is valuable when you want to obscure responsibility to soften a negative communication.

An easy trick: Use passives in combination with an "It is . . ." or "It was . . ." or "It will be . . ." opening, to avoid responsibility while still making your point:

- "It is anticipated that . . ."
- "It has been suggested that . . ."

These exceptions give us a reason for considering passive voice. Most of us who write for a living don't like passives because they invariably have less impact. But switching to passive voice is an easy way to reposition the limelight, an example of the first exception:

"I accepted the job" puts me in first position and the job in second position. "The job was offered to me" puts the job in first position and me in second position. Depending on where the writer wants to put primary emphasis, active may give way to passive.

Example of the second exception:

Your subscription to WYOMING OUTDOORS has been suspended for non-payment. To reinstate it, send payment immediately. A postage-free envelope has been provided for this purpose.

We have two passives here. Compare this message with the same information put entirely in the active voice:

We have suspended your subscription to WYOMING OUTDOORS for non-payment. To reinstate it, send payment immediately. We have enclosed a postage-free envelope for this purpose.

This message has been packed in favor of passives. (Note, please: The previous sentence is passive. Why?) For example, this copy says "We have" instead of "We've" because this active construction is closest to the more formal passive voice. But even if the copy said, "We've had to suspend your subscription . . ." it would have been more severe than the passive approach because it's a one-on-one finger-pointing statement.

Passive voice avoids the *"J'accuse"* posture. Is this good? Maybe. It's one more deliberate decision the alert communicator makes.

Using ". . . ing" to Add Power

A mild grammatical trick: Using a gerund form of a word—
". . .ing"—makes an action more personal and imminent.
Compare these two versions of the same statement:

> *I suggest you switch your auto insurance to our
> company.*

or—

> *I'm suggesting you switch your auto insurance to our
> company.*

or, to double the "ing" effect—

> *I'm suggesting you consider switching your auto
> insurance to our company.*

The first "ing," appended to the word *suggest*, makes our
suggestion more timely. "I'm suggesting" is *now*, while "I suggest"
is timeless. The second "ing," appended to the word *switch* (with
consider added to avoid illiteracy), masks our aggressive salesmanship.

The standard caution in these pages: Don't assume the
dynamic is always the best road. Effective copy carries the reader
at a controlled pace. Sometimes we speed, and sometimes we
tarry to sightsee. Knowing when to speed up and when to slow
down is what separates powerful copywriters from our competent
but less-aware competitors.

Another advantage of "ing": The action appears to be contin-
uous. "We receive many requests for information" is ongoing but

not an unbroken line. "We are receiving many requests for information" seems to be endless. (The ". . . ing" form has more
power, but the statements aren't totally parallel, so each has its
uses.)

Inconsequential nits—*that, it,* ". . .ing,*" occasional passive
voice—these are the separators enabling master communicators
to maintain their ongoing edge over those who either don't know
or don't care that differences do exist.

Chapter 10
The Blah and the Weak

Writing around a point and apologizing are twisted 180 degrees from the concept of Power Communication.

Neutral words don't motivate. They're out of the power communicator's vocabulary.

Apologies don't motivate. They suggest you're weaker than the person you're trying to convince. Who will buy from a weak salesperson?

Writers and speakers who lard their messages with meaningless pomposities such as *utilize* and *receive* inflict termite-like damage on their messages. The structure weakens, invisibly at first, then noticeably as air replaces substance.

Chapter 3 covered the way little words can effect a profound change to the impact not only of a message but a single sentence. This chapter—"The Blah and the Weak"—encompasses both implicitly weak individual words and the philosophical whole.

The Peripheral Pussyfooting Weakener

Writing around a point drains excitement.

That's the first half of a rule, The Peripheral Pussyfooting Weakener. Let's look at the second half of the rule.

Visualize a setting: Into a sedate roomful of dinner guests bursts a breathless messenger. He gasps out:

*A short distance down the road, our bellicose
opponents can't go unnoticed. Within a short period of
time our defenses may be breached by hostile troops.*

The message is dire, but the delivery is flat. How much more
dramatic, as long as he's gasping anyway, to pant an exclamation:

The enemy is coming!

So we form the rule to cover those thoughtless circumstances
in which, dignity-driven, we forget why we're at the keyboard in
the first place. ***The Peripheral Pussyfooting Weakener Rule*** can
keep us from lapsing into punchless prose:

> ■ Writing around a point drains excitement out. A
> message loses impact in direct ratio to the percent-
> age of information given indirectly instead of
> directly.

Example? How about this line from a communication in, sadly,
an advertising publication:

At the proper time, good things will happen.

When is the proper time? What good things?
We all have written thoughtless word strings like that; but
no more, not with knowledge of the Peripheral Pussyfooting
Weakener haunting our brains. If you have the time right now,
analyze and rewrite this mushy sentence. Assuming it refers to a
newspaper switching to non-bleed inks, a week from Sunday,
write a single sentence transmitting its message *directly* instead of
indirectly.
Why go through that exercise? Because you could have a

Fig. 10.1

"Quality" is a neutral word, in the same colorless family as "service" and "value." A graciously upscale intimation (such as "affluence" or "prosperity" or "real substance") might have had greater power, especially in a reference to four million subscribers.

parallel sentence squatting, near-invisible, in a piece of prose you're writing right now.

Negative Synergism: The Generalization-Weakener

Adding generalizations weakens a statement. A bank advertises:

Our dollars are helping Milltown grow.

Okay, the sentence is a cliché. But weak as it is, it still is stronger than it becomes when we tack a rotted plank onto its end:

Our dollars are helping your town grow, by serving every one of your banking needs.

We might call this *negative synergism*—one-half multiplied by one-half equals one-quarter.

We can learn from vaudeville: When you're stuck without an exit line, get offstage as quickly and gracefully as you can.

The Genteel Word-Choice Weakener

Plain talk is more emotion-charged than genteel word-choice. This was the wording of a fund-raising mailing:

What if we had to close down for lack of funds?

Funds are fiduciary. *Money* is gutty. If we're shaking the potential contributor, changing the word adds wallop:

What if we had to close down for lack of money?

When we fine-tune words, replacement adds a touch of impact here and a feather of weight there. Instead of—

Lift the phone and . . .

we write—

Pick up the phone and . . .

A disclaimer here: Some "upscale" copy demands genteel words in order to preserve verisimilitude. *Dine* is more genteel than *eat,* but dine is what we do in a fancy restaurant. The point: Your decision to use or discard genteel words should be conscious, not unconscious.

Word-tuning is like harnessing a chihuahua to help pull the sled. It might not help much, but it won't hurt.

The "Definition" Weakener

Don't have your words "define" when they can "assume."

Accomplishing this isn't as tricky as the wording suggests. It's a variation on the standard negative reaction by aggressive communicators to the "accountant mentality" which equates defining a problem with doing something about it.

We look at what appears to be a perfectly acceptable sentence:

This is a masterpiece which will attract every eye when you display it in your home or office.

If we remember our roles as *force*-communicators, we spot a weakness in the fabric. The line *defines* where it just as easily could sell for us:

These Guys Ha
Could Wind Up Wi

A right fielder challenges to lead the league in RBIs and is compar
young Ted Williams. A center fielder steals six bases in one game, establis
a modern-day record. A former second baseman relegated to the minors ret
rule the outfield like it's his own backyard. All play for an underdog team in the m

Fig. 10.2
Purely masculine, this ad not only uses a baseball player as its illustration but begins with "These Guys"—macho terminology. One obvious problem: the ad is aimed at <u>advertisers</u>, not sports addicts. Lack of marketing specifics may generate another buyer conclusion: the writer <u>deliberately</u> avoided explicit references to ratings.

Many Hits They
eir Own Fall Series.

a Cinderella comeback. And a race for the National League pennant.

A hot new Hollywood screenplay? Not at all. More like history in the making. It's Braves Baseball on TBS. And it's the perfect investment for your advertising dollars, because millions of fans of the Great American Pastime are watching America's Team as it beats the odds.

TBS

*This masterpiece will attract every eye when you
display it in your home or office.*

Should you inspect every sentence for *which* and *that* phrases?
It depends on how much of a purist you are . . . and how much
loose time you have. (See *That*-Bashing Revisited," chapter 9.)

The Conditional Weakener

Don't unnecessarily inject a condition. Exercise **The Rule of
Condition Injection-Rejection**:

- Conditions weaken a message.

Why shoot yourself in the foot? Suggesting the reader may
or may not have the ability to respond to our message gives that
reader an opportunity to escape.

A sentence in a high-powered letter reads:

*We have arranged for a relative handful of subscribers
to be able to obtain this book on the same advantageous
terms our own members enjoy.*

The wormy apple in this word-barrel is "be able." What does
it add to the selling argument other than *condition*? So we change
the sentence to—

*We have arranged for a relative handful of subscribers
to obtain this book on the same advantageous terms
our own members enjoy.*

Conditions have their place, as qualifiers. *Ability* to participate, to perform, to qualify . . . these are valuable components of
exclusivity, one of the great motivators of this decade. But when
we don't need a qualifier, we don't need a condition.

Chrome-Plate Your Nuts and Bolts

A simple way to enhance descriptions: Choose the least nuts-and-bolts-like terminology. Inside the office we call those sticky things on car windows *decals*; to customers they're *transfers*. Inside the office we call a continuity program a *series*; to potential collectors, it's a *collection* . . . no, a *Collection*, because capitalizing adds importance.

The Rule of Capitalization:

- Capitalize for importance.

"I invite you to become a member of The Advisory Board of The Turmeric Society" carries greater distinction than "I invite you to become a member of the advisory board of the Turmeric Society."

Inside the office we talk about "while supplies last"; to targets, we say, "Until our limited allotment is exhausted." Think of what impresses the reader, not what a bookkeeper might enter in a ledger.

Popular Isn't Motivational

The car dealer knows his business. When a prospect walks in, one look tells the dealer: This guy either wants to be mainstream or wants individuality. "This is our most popular model" turns that prospect on or off.

Popular doesn't suggest exclusivity and can damage an upscale pitch. *Desirable* or *sought after* is better for this effect. A "popular" style may, in fact, decrease interest of the most sophisticated buyers. A more classic example: two women wearing identical gowns at the Opera Ball. Can you imagine either of them being happy—with her choice or with the store?

Phony Stroking

The highest-level targets respond most negatively to phony stroking.

A mailing headed "Because you're an intelligent traveler . . ." is more likely to irritate this group than it would a group which *doesn't* regard itself as intelligent travelers. Better:

"Because you're an experienced traveler . . ."

"Experienced" relates to *background* rather than *mental capacity*. An upscale individual outside your orbit is more logically likely to take a negative point of view toward your assumption of mental capacity than toward your assumption of background.

Nobody Needs "Needs"

An automatic way to inject strength into any communication is to look through it and replace every use of the word *needs* as a noun.

A personal prejudice? Not prejudice; recognition.

This author regards the would-be communicator who depends on *needs* as a Yellow Pages reject.

(For those who haven't run afoul of this ancient prejudice, the explanation/justification for the author's disdain is the completely nondescriptive nature of this running-in-place word. Uncreative local insurance agents run Yellow Pages ads headed "For All Your Insurance Needs"; digit-headed computer stores run ads headed "For All Your Computer Needs.")

(What these noncommunications really say is, "I don't know what you want, Mister, so please write my ad for me.")

Analyze your reaction to the heading of this self-mailer:

The 1025 R/E Marathon
Copier . . . it expands to
meet your needs.

The versatile Xerox 1025 R/E Marathon Copier may be
the only copier you'll ever need. It comes with big
copier features, such as reduction and enlargement at 8
settings. And the 1025 R/E is tough to outgrow—even
as your business expands—because you can add up to
8 different combinations of features any time you need
them.

Not terrible. Just muzzy. And the reader doesn't appreciate
having the first-cousin word *need* in there twice, plus *tough* in a
context he has to reinterpret. The reader might have been willing
to forget the whole thing until reading the last sentence in that
column:

Just choose the model that suits your present and
future office needs.

The word *need* appears three more times in the short copy
block. The reader wonders which was more offbeat: the writer's
happy fascination with the word or the message recipient's implicit
annoyance with its lack of specificity.

Repeated-Word Weakeners . . .
And How to Make Them Not So Weak

Using the same key word twice in the same sentence is an
unnecessary contribution to incoherence.

Fig. 10.3
Relying on "needs" as a noun robs a headline of power. Because the bullet copy has specifics, it would have made a better heading. Also, ending a non-exclamatory statement with an exclamation point ("For Quality and Reliability at competitive prices contact us today!") makes the appeal shrill and desperate.

This doesn't apply to *a, an,* or *the.* It applies only occasionally to *that.* The target is any less-common word which appears a second time before the reader's brain has flushed the first appearance.

A subscription letter begins:

Dear Member:

One of the many advantages of membership in the American Museum of Natural History is the opportunity to take advantage of the many benefits available to you when you join.

The "Huh?" reaction to the apparent incoherence of this thought is enhanced by the double use of the word "advantage": One of the advantages is the opportunity to take advantage . . .

We suffer the same feeling of frustration we get when we

look for a definition in the dictionary and find the same word.

But the subhead for this section promises to tell us "how to make them not so weak." Okay, how?

Easy. *The Rule of Key Word Repetition*:

■ If you have to re-use a word in speech or writing, emphasize the key word before its second use to show the reader the repeat is intentional.

The *key* word before its *second* use . . . this is one of those wonderful semi-trivial tips linking the mechanical with the creative. Implementing it requires nothing except a couple of digs at the "search" key.

Suppose in re-reading something you've written you see something like this:

I know you've seen art masterpieces before. But this is really an art masterpiece.

Aside from the flatness of this approach, we've lost impact because the word "masterpiece" appears twice. So we try it this way:

I know you've seen art masterpieces before. But this is *really* an art masterpiece.

In a letter, "really" is underlined; in typeset, it's italic (no boldface, please—it looks ridiculous). In speech, it's greater volume or a higher sound. This example and the words in it are inconsequential; what matters is clarifying the communicator's deliberate re-use of the word.

Clarification includes choosing which of two words in a repeated phrase to give emphatic treatment—"He always has lived well. Now he lives *so* well people wonder where the money comes from."

When as a First-Word Weakener

Chapter 3 discusses a little word with many uses and many misuses—*when*. A quick look at *when* from another dimension.

Sometimes eliminating *when* as the first word of a sentence adds strength. Look for surplus when-constructions such as, "[When] asked what advice he would give young executives . . . "

Don't interpret this suggestion as implication that all when-words are surplus. Use it as reinforcement for the truism: *Good writing is lean.*

Understand Is Weaker Than "Figure Out"

"I understand" (or "Do you understand?") is passive and therefore less emphatic than "I figured it out" (or "Have you figured it out?").

"Figuring out" is more reader-involving, implying more active participation than *understand*, which suggests acceptance.

"Don't Have Any . . ." Is Weaker Than "Have No . . ."

"Have no . . ." is more desperate than "don't have any . . .":
"They have no food" is a more despairing circumstance than "They don't have any food."

When I come to work...
I come to <u>work</u>!

Fig. 10.4

The Rule of Key Word Repetition suggests emphasizing the key word before the second use of a repeated word. In this instance, lacking a key word before the second use, emphasizing the second use itself is the right way to make a point. Visualize this message without underlining the second "work." Impact would have been negligible.

Why? Because "They don't have any food" doesn't generate the thought of a permanent condition. The target individual isn't slapped with the thought of desperation: They don't have any *at this moment.*

"They have no food" is absolute and unconditional.

Use "have no" for fund-raising, for cries of help, for flat statements of components or ingredients (see "Can Negatives Be Positives?" chapter 6). Use "don't have any" when you want to suggest a condition with the capability of change.

"Of The . . ." Can Weaken . . . or Specify

"Of the . . ." can be a weakener, but it also can be a specifier. This makes it worth checking.

Eliminate "of the" when you're sure the elimination is because you want to be *less* specific. **Example:**

> *"Some of the planes have individual TV sets."*

or—

> *"Some planes have individual TV sets."*

The first is weaker, but it specifies a group of planes; the second is stronger but indefinite.

Automatic Weakeners: "Some Of" and Other Assembly Words

The point has been made: Qualifiers are weakeners. This is one of the obvious differences between unprofessional and professional copy.

Or is it so obvious? The writer of a subscription mailing either forgot it or was unaware of it when writing this:

You'll lose some of your benefits.

This copy suggests you'll still have some benefits. Why do this, when a publication is engaged in the titanic struggle to get a renewal? Far better is the same sentence without the weakener:

You'll lose benefits.

This same communication had this line:

I've enclosed a list of your previous subscriptions . . .

For action, the writer is better off bringing the relationship into the present tense:

I've enclosed a list of your subscriptions.

"Assembly" words seldom are the best choices for projecting the image of style, class, or exclusivity. Assembly words are words such as *group* or *some* or *many* or *quantity* or *comprised*. So the editor who saw this copy—

These miniature cakes are comprised of some of the world's most expensive liqueurs . . .

and changed it to—

These miniature cakes include a carefully chosen group of the world's most expensive liqueurs . . .

did only half a job. To clean out the assembly words, that editor should have figured a way to get rid of *include* and *group*:

> *A carefully chosen selection of the world's most*
> *expensive liqueurs impart their flavors to these*
> *miniature cakes . . .*

Replacing assembly words isn't a big deal. It won't resurrect a crashing empire. But, like one fire ant in a mob of fire ants, it adds a little more impact. And our job is just that: to add impact where we can and *never* to sap away impact.

Oxymorons and Morons: Weakness From Mismatched Words

Suppose this text told you that many hundreds of the top direct marketers have written, faxed, or called, telling how much they appreciate the concept of Power Communication.

Your logical rebuttal: "Aha! Gotcha!"

How right you would be. Right out of *Hamlet*, the author would be hoist with his own petard. He'd have violated a principle of power communication by the very phrase, "many hundreds of the top direct marketers."

Get it? The statement declared exclusivity and denied it in the same phrase. The word "hundreds" is the culprit. Without it—"Many of the top direct marketers"—we have a phrase that survives, weak though it is from lack of specificity.

Deliberate oxymorons can create a memorable sense of uniqueness; inadvertent oxymorons can bite you.

For those who don't know the term, an oxymoron combines two contradicting words into a single phrase: "Wise fool" is not only an oxymoron; it explains the word itself, *oxys* being ancient Greek for *sharp* and *moron* meaning just what it means today.

Tongue-in-cheekers say that word-combinations such as *legal ethics* or *government efficiency* or *military intelligence* or *postal service* are oxymorons, because in each instance the two words are an impossible combination.

From these we can get *The Oxymoron Reaction Rule*:

- When your oxymoron causes a double-take, you're a winner. When people laugh at your oxymoron— and you didn't intend to generate laughter—you're a loser.

Years ago Revlon shook up the world of cosmetics with a product-line called "Fire and Ice"—an oxymoron. The arthritis rub "Icy Hot" is a current oxymoron. "Where Business Is a Pleasure" is a mild oxymoron, as is "The Birth of a Legend."

Less convincing is "A New Family Heirloom," too tortured and contrived to be effective. "Old New Mexico" has a peculiar ring to it.

A classic violation of The Oxymoron Reaction Rule is a direct mail letter signed by the head of a collectibles company:

As chairman of the [NAME] Collection, I am privileged to see many rare works of art.

Competitors are eager (check the word *eager* because we'll come to it in two paragraphs) to shoot us in the foot. Let's not do it to ourselves. A Power Communicator would have spotted the gaffe—how can "many" coexist with "rare"?—and quickly rewritten the statement for coherence:

Fig. 10.5

In the wrong hands, humor can make the writer seem amateurish and sophomoric. In the right hands, it can reach and influence readers, viewers, or listeners who ignore traditional messages. This is humor adeptly handled. Note that if this ad were run in repeated issues of the magazine, its impact would decline at a considerably faster rate than one might expect of more conventional advertising.

Fig. 10.6

Was this writer trying to be funny? If so, the humor was poorly aimed, because the suggestion that a job-seeker can get a top position through "b.s." is the exact opposite of what this university is selling. I find it difficult to believe that the writer used "b.s." innocently, not knowing the common use of these initials.

*As chairman of the [NAME] Collection, every now
and then I am privileged to see a rare work of art.*

Now, how about *eager*?

Simple enough. *Eager* and *anxious aren't* parallel. Want proof? Extend the words. *Eagerness* and *anxiety* show the difference between a word with a positive overtone and a word with a negative overtone. Had the wording been, "Competitors are anxious to shoot us in the foot," their image changes from slathering competitors to worriers looking for a way out of their inferior position.

Because *eager* has a positive connotation and *anxious* has a negative connotation, "I'm eager to see this show" can't stand an *anxious* replacement. In fact, anxiety might be left to the producer: "I'm anxious about this show."

Say What You Mean: Slack = Weak

Think the way good salespeople think: They keep the word strings tight. Slack = weak. So to move the reader or listener off his emotional duff, say what you mean.

A seminar mailing to personnel executives had this sentence:

*The intent is greater corporate image-enhancement
from every person who attends this seminar.*

Okay, we see an immediate flaw, and it's a common one in seminar mailings: The writer has substituted intellectual words for emotional words.

Do you see another problem? The writer hasn't said what he or she means. What *is* "image-enhancement"? The reader may have a muddy idea, but the idea doesn't draw a word picture. It doesn't give the reader a reason to enroll in this seminar.

What if we stitched in this alteration?

The purpose is greater profit-making capability for you—from every employee you send to this seminar.

Let's count the differences.

1. "Purpose" is a more emotional word than "intent." Score one for us.
2. "Profit-making capability" is specific, and "image-enhancement" is general. Score two for us.
3. The mailing was to personnel executives; ". . . every person who attends . . ." doesn't suggest a *you* action, but ". . . every employee you send . . ." does. Score three for us.

A local radio station had this throwaway:

Coming up: Late news for your listening pleasure.

"Pleasure"? Is that why people listen to the news? We listen to music, comedy, drama, and maybe even talk shows for pleasure. The word draws no image when used to describe news. Radio stations have only one communications weapon: sound. Most of their sounds are words. This radio station needs to sharpen its weapons.

Is all this trivial? Probably . . . but we're back to the nonexistent weight difference between a pound of iron and a pound of feathers. We don't have a big deal here, but we have a mini-point to consider whenever we're trying to motivate—which if we make our livings as communicators is 101% of the time.

Depersonalized Weakeners

Depersonalizers are weakeners.

The first shot in a communication is crucial. It establishes a personalized tie or it begins a thin rhetorical hemophilia.

A magazine looking for advertisers removed itself from its own sales argument with this first line of the sales letter:

1991 was a year that showed great progress.

If your reaction to this limp opening is "So what?" you're in the majority. "We made great progress in 1991" at least ties the meaningless line to *somebody*; "Most companies in your field made great progress in 1991. Did you?" hurls down a gauntlet that should inspire the recipient to read on.

Vagueness and Statistics = Weakness

Vague words dampen involvement. Statistics dampen involvement.

A fund-raising mailing has this highlighted sentence:

Around 2.5 million hungry people in the two western regions of Sudan will soon run out of food.

Can you see three separate problems with this sentence?

Based on the subhead for this section you may see two. What's the third? Let's count:

1. The word "Around" not only is nonspecific but indicates a lack of concern. It's an outsider's term, not a concerned insider's.

2. The number "2.5 million" is a statistician's number, not a humanitarian's.
3. "Run out of food" is a mechanical conclusion, not a Samaritan's whose concern isn't running out of food but going hungry.

Diminutives Diminish Seriousness and Increase Rapport . . . Sometimes Good, Sometimes Bad

Apparent attitudinal seriousness diminishes with use of shortened or abbreviated forms of words.

"He has the flu" is less serious than "He has influenza." One reason doctors and lawyers make miserable dinner party seatmates is their insistence on using long or formal terms. Nobody ever has a bruise; it's a hematoma. And who but a lawyer would use "Whereas" in conversation?

"Have you considered whether you can telephone the company carrying your automobile insurance?" is a more formal presentation than the more casual "Have you considered whether you can phone the company carrying your car insurance?"

Hold it, please: This isn't militating for informality. It just points out the *option*. The difference between formal and informal has value both ways. When we're buddying up to our target, we very well might want to use *phone* and *car*.

Do we use *TV* or *television*? Do we refer to an *ad* or an *advertisement*? Is this "The United States" or "The United States of America"?

Remember the 1988 presidential campaign? Political analysts agree that Michael Dukakis appeared stiff-necked by constantly formalizing his rhetoric. He kept using the longer term, "The United States of America"; and during a televised debate, when

George Bush called CNN anchorman Bernard Shaw "Bernie," Dukakis doggedly maintained arm's length by calling him "Bernard." Guess who won?

But hold it again. The Master Point of all power communication is to match the message to the target. So whether we use *photo* or *photograph* doesn't depend on whether we're implicitly a Dukakis or a Bush. It depends on how professional we are at recognizing and matching our targets-of-the-moment.

Reaction to Words Determines Involvement

Communicators shouldn't need this rule, but since it exists, let's tuck *The Dynamic Reaction Rule* into our rhetorical hip-pocket:

- If you want to generate a dynamic reaction, use dynamic words. If you want to generate an observer reaction, use colorless words.

When might you want to generate an observer reaction? Two circumstances:

1. When you're describing a competitor's product or services and don't want to be overtly derogatory;
2. When you're being instructional and want to avoid provoking a viewpoint.

Those exceptions represent a fraction of the power communicator's transmissions. Usually, within the orbit, we ferret out and replace random weakeners.

An example of a communicator's casual or ignorant disregard of the Dynamic Reaction Rule is this statement, lifted from a computer service company's solicitation:

We'll send you a written purchase order.

It's harmless enough. It's descriptive. It's precise. So what's wrong with it?

From the viewpoint of most wordsmiths, nothing. But that's because so often we forget why we're hired: to generate a dynamic reaction, not just an uninvolved reader reaction.

Look what happens when we change one word:

We'll send you a signed purchase order.

The difference between a written purchase order (uninvolved) and a signed purchase order (involved) might not result in one additional response. On the other hand, it might. So isn't it worth switching words?

Power Communication Is Never Having to Say, "I'm Sorry"

You never have a valid reason for apologizing in a communication intended to persuade the message recipient to take a positive action.

A direct response service company starts its *unsolicited* sales letter this way:

We're sorry these pictures aren't "professionally glossy," but we wanted to get this information to you right away. . . .

What salesman in his right mind would ever start a pitch with "I'm sorry"? How much more thoughtful the copy would be if it started out:

I couldn't wait!

No, I couldn't wait for the professional photographer to show up to take some "glamour" shots. So I grabbed my own instant-camera to make it possible for me to show you fast. . . .

Effective power communication, like effective courtship, is never having to say, "I'm sorry."

"Mother, May I?"

The word *may* is worth a search-key hunt because of its self-destruct potential.

We aren't discussing the difference between *Can* and *May*; if we haven't mastered third-grade grammar and as communicators learned which rules to ignore, we shouldn't be reading this book.

What we *are* discussing are the overtones to the word *may*, which can backfire on us:

- *May* suggests "or may not."
- *May* suggests permission.

It's a subtle point, but it's one we should look for when we're creating response devices. Have you ever written a sentence such as this, which appeared in the middle of a response device in a mailing for a telephone system for small offices?

I may spread my payments over 24 months.

The children's game "Mother, May I" flashes. Here we are,

trying to get an order, and the word *may* says to the reader, softly and even subliminally:

1. You haven't yet made a decision; you may . . . or you may not.
2. We're giving you permission.

Sure, there are times when suggesting not-yet or giving permission is a potent selling weapon, but this isn't one of them. Subliminal or not, why take a chance? So we change the sentence to—

I have the option of spreading the payments over 24 months.

Same thing, but this revision avoids the uncertainties of *may*.

When to Use "Who is . . ." and "Which Is . . ."

Use the phrase "who is . . ." or "which is . . ." to identify a person, item, or circumstance you assume the person to whom you're communicating *doesn't* know. Don't use the phrase if you assume the reader does know.

"Who is" and "which is" are overused. They parallel a speaker saying "Uhhhh" while trying to think of the next line. So, generally, leave them out. This is a subtle point, but check the difference:

John Jones, who is the local dog-catcher, says he has oodles of poodles.

or—

John Jones, the local dog-catcher, says he has oodles of poodles.

See the difference? The "who is" is *deliberately explanatory*, assuming no prior knowledge of who John Jones is. Without the two words, the writer says to the communications target, "We both know Jones."

Choose the inclusion or exclusion of "who is" on this basis, and the reader reacts to the identification as you want him/her to react.

Generally, try to get rid of "which is" and "which are" as descriptives. (They're useful in questions: "Which is the one you want?" . . . "Who are those people?") What do the words add to statements such as—"This new development, [which is] preferred by every major industrial user . . ."; "Our bank, [which is] located on the corner of Fifth and Main . . ."?

(For verbalisms such as broadcast, don't use "who is" at all. The verbalized version is, "John Jones—he's the local dog catcher—says he has oodles of poodles.")

Humor: For Professionals Only

Humor is a dangerous tool. Proof is the number of times a "funny" advertisement wins an award but fails to sell anything.

Exception: A *deliberately* ridiculous statement which places the reader in a self-mocking "in-group" can build rapport better than exhortation.

This may seem impenetrable, without an example. If you regularly bypass *exclusivity* as a motivator, it doesn't have much value to you. To those who know how easy it is to use exclusivity as a motivator, but who too often tumble over the brink of shrillness, it's a merry road to camaraderie.

A mailing from a company called Caviarteria has this legend on its face:

THE TERRIFYING
PROSPECT OF A
CAVIAR SHORTAGE
And How We Are
Planning to Cope . . .

Even the Prince of Monaco wouldn't be terrified by the prospect of a caviar shortage. Do you see what this writer did? By poking fun at epicurean tastes, he or she makes us want to be part of this group.

Warning: Save this technique for items or services fitting into a genuine key-club "I'm a carefree snob and so are you" mold.

Weeding Out the Weaklings

The difference between a tortuous discipline and an automatic knee-jerk reaction: *practice.*

Those who coach executives in speech-making techniques have a technique of their own: If the speaker has an "Uhhh" habit or starts too many thoughts with "Now" or "Well," the coaches tape-record a presentation, then edit the transgressions into a single string. This shock therapy usually creates such hyperawareness of the failing that the speaker is jolted out of the addiction forever.

The communicator can be his or her own therapist. *Un*-learning communication weakness brings spontaneous communication strength.

Chapter 11
Which Person Should It Be?

You has been the key word in effective advertising and sales
promotion since Biblical times. (If you missed it, Chapter 3
suggests: "Look for ways to inject *you* into the word mix.")

Civilization has moved a long way—in an oblique direction
—from "Blessed are the pure in heart." Today's businessperson
and clergyperson both know a great marketing truth:

> *To our target, a product or service is less what it* is
> *than what the target thinks it* does—*for him or her.*

So "You" becomes the marketing nucleus. This explains the
success of the salesperson who doesn't know the stock, doesn't
know mechanical specifics, and doesn't even care about technical
orientation . . . but outsells everyone else on the sales staff. This
guy knows how to inject *you* into the sales pitch, and this injection
far outweighs any technical orientation or expertise.

"You" keeps your appeal personal. So, so many communications begin with flat reader-*un*involving statements.
Example:

> *People are always asking me if vitamins are needed.*
> *The answer is not just a matter of my opinion, but of*
> *fact.*

The reader yawns. "So what?"

Visualize that same opening, with a quick 90-degree involve-
ment-turn added:

People are always asking me if vitamins are needed.
How about you? Do you think they are?

We've added a basic involvement device. We use "those people" as a foil for the reader. Without the comparative or some other "they/you" relationship, an impersonal opening is ice cold. Warming it up requires no more talent than asking, "Have I involved the person at whom I aimed this message?"

A sidebar is *The Rule of "Importance" Projection*:

- A scream of importance loses impact in ratio to the dominance of "We" references over "You" references following the scream.

"In Loco Parentis" Can Mean a "Plumb Loco" Parent

The Latin phrase "in loco parentis" means one person puts himself in the position of parent to another. Teachers, clergymen, dictators, benevolent bosses, and actual parents can pull this off. Acting like a parent when you're trying to convince a skeptic can have you in the wastebasket or on a dead channel within seconds.

This gives us *The "Mother, May I?" Rule:*

- Don't play "Mother, May I?" with your target unless he or she is preconditioned to accept you as a superior.

Who are we to grant permission to somebody who neither knows us, nor cares about us, nor has any fealty to us? We've all been exposed and even overexposed to the two differences between *can* and *may*—the difference in standard English usage and the difference in our force-communication messages (see "'Can' and Its Confrères," Chapter 3).

If I'm selling you something you *must* have, I just *may* let you get one. But if I'm in the normal selling posture, hawking my wares to somebody who never heard of me, I'm better off stroking than suggesting personal mastery.

A power communicator wouldn't, for example, have used this as the final sentence in a "Johnson Box" (in a direct response letter, that rectangular box above the greeting, bordered by stars or asterisks . . . whose value in initiating a positive impact is questionable) to start a letter:

> *You may receive your first issue FREE*
> *with no risk or obligation to continue.*

No, it isn't a big deal; it's a minor irritant that jarred the recipient, and we can (not *may*) assume it jarred—subliminally, but so what?—readers. Why not keep the juices flowing with, "I'll send your first issue FREE . . ."?

If "You're One" Then "I'm One Too"

Saying "I'm one too" eliminates the patronizing tone of a "preachy" communication and the embarrassment attending a message whose subject is the reader's handicap, shortcoming, or deficiency. It builds immediate reader rapport.

Which of these openings is less likely to be tossed into the wastebasket?

- Dear Art Lover
- Dear Fellow Art Lover

This is a "soft" example: No one objects to being described as an art lover; the value here is avoidance of a patronizing attitude.

A "hard" example—"Dear Fellow Victim of [WHATEVER]"—indicates how including yourself becomes valuable when marketing personal products designed to mask or overcome a problem.

When and How to Increase the Degree of Imperative

The Rule of Increasing Imperative:

■ The degree of imperative can increase as the text of a communication to those who aren't captive readers or listeners progresses.

This point can be helpful in structuring a sales letter to cold lists (those who haven't done business with you before). As an opener, "I think you'll be interested in this news" is less abrasive than "You'll be interested in this news" or "You should be interested in this news."

Obviously, to *captive* readers or listeners—such as members of an organization, co-religionists, or those who acknowledge a common cause—"You should be interested in this news" is a more effective opener, because the communicator establishes his/her own position by an authoritarian statement.

As the p.s., *after* presenting a seemingly logical proposition, an imperative is in order: "I [think] [hope] I've proved to you: You should be interested in this news."

Claiming Proprietorship: Right or Wrong?

Claiming proprietorship at the wrong time can exclude a potential buyer. Introducing a possessive too soon can damage credibility.

Our is best used to refer to the "Triple-P"—procedures, people, and position. Using *our* for something you're trying to sell keeps the prospect out.

So we look at this sentence—

Our Reservatron Reservation System is specifically created for municipal special events.

and we see the hole in the fabric. It's *their* system, and we're on the outside. Changing the first word—

The Reservatron Reservation System is specifically created for municipal special events.

enables us to participate. We aren't outsiders. (See chapter 6, "The Difference Between 'If You're Not' and 'If You Aren't'," to see why "We aren't outsiders" is more appropriate here than "We're not outsiders.")

As a letter greeting, "To Our Very Special Customer" is presumptuous. Start with "To a Very Special Customer," then add possessive and exclusivity in the letter-text.

Don't interpret these suggestions to mean *our* is a dangerous word. Interpret it to mean we're in a selling posture. Including the reader or listener is the head-to-head salesperson's automatic spear; too-early assumption of ownership can blunt that spear.

The "We" to "You" Tie

Having the reader think the writer is God is a sign of high professionalism. Having the reader think the writer thinks *he's* God is a torn relationship.

In this Age of Skepticism pontificating and preaching aren't "in" even for the Sunday morning sermon. The writer can avoid the reader's objection to a dramatically projected point by starting with three little words: "We both know. . . ."

Building Rapport by Assuming a Proprietary Relationship

Assuming a proprietary relationship builds rapport.

Suppose you're trying to resuscitate former customers. Which greeting do you think will be a better emotional grabber?

To A Former Customer,

or—

To Our Former Customer,

"Our" is proprietary. It isn't presumptuous; it's a statement of relationship, implicitly warm. We've already discussed the indefinite article *a* (chapter 4) as the least personal adjective in the lexicon.

In this usage *Our* doesn't establish arm's-length proprietorship; it parallels *you* and *your* in confirming the mutuality of our connection. It establishes affinity, tying us together. *A* helps widen the gulf that must exist or we wouldn't be *former* customers.

If you've swallowed that one, take one more look at "To Our Former Customer," and consider the punctuation mark at the end.

A colon at the end of a greeting is crisp and businesslike. A comma is casual and personal.

Most business letters use a colon and most personal letters use a comma. If we know that, it's no ball game. We use a comma.

So it isn't—

To Our Former Customer:

instead, it's—

To Our Former Customer,

Don't mistake the colon after a greeting for a colon in ongoing textual use. The crispness of a colon has a purpose in force-communication: It tells the reader the statement following it will add impact to the statement before it (as, with any good luck, this statement just did).

The Value of Third-Person Outrage

Third-person outrage is more effective than first-person outrage when the writer wants reader acceptance of a negative situation.

"The IRS took everything I own—even my furniture" can be construed as caterwauling. "The IRS took everything he owned—even his furniture" is third-person outrage. A reader or listener is more likely to believe the outrage when it's reported by an apparently unbiased observer.

Why The Rationale Can't Equal the Offer

If you've been trying to overpower a prospective buyer or convince a business associate or potential love partner to see it your way, without notable success, gear-switching may be in order. *The Me-Myself-I Rule:*

- Your quarries care about themselves, not you; so
  get to the benefits fast.

For advertisers, the reason some mailings fail (it's less true
of space and broadcast ads) is the writer's assumption that the
rationale is as interest-grabbing as the offer. Sorry, no. In fact, we
can add a Rule to the grab bag of helpful hints we've been collect-
ing, by reversing this misconception 180 degrees. We then have
The Argumentative Supremacy Truism:

- "What's in it for me?" is paramount, over any other
  component of the sales argument. To the message-
  recipient, the rationale behind the offer is inconsequential.

Let's apply the Argumentative Supremacy Truism to the fund
raising mailing whose letter begins this way:

Dear Friend,

> *It is my pleasure, on behalf of the Officers
> and Directors, to invite you to join the American
> Horticultural Society as a National Member.*

> *This national non-profit organization is, as you
> probably know, the center for gardening and gardeners
> in the United States.*

> *As a member, you will enjoy unique and
> valuable benefits. And you will be part of a highly
> influential group working quietly and effectively for
> goals I know you share.*

The American Horticultural Society is all these things, and more:

. . . A national clearing house for horticultural knowledge, bringing you extraordinarily useful information.

. . . A meeting ground for discerning gardeners, both amateur and professional.

. . . A force for environmental protection, conservation, horticultural research and development, and the preservation of natural beauty.

Well, you get the idea. This letter's key selling argument is *rationale*, not *what's in it for you*. It suffers. Rationale works only with the hard-core in-group.

For example, the third paragraph begins, "As a member, you will enjoy unique and valuable benefits." Okay, just what *are* those benefits? (While we're in that paragraph, being part of a group "working quietly and effectively for goals . . ." is a turnoff. Who wants to work, especially since this suggests we won't get any individual recognition? Cynical as it may seem, the Argumentative Supremacy Truism applies here too.)

The Advantage of Apparent Proprietorship

Injecting a sense of target proprietorship can be contagious. The communicator says, "Your." The reader or listener thinks, "Mine."

No, it isn't that simple or foolproof because it's just another power communications effect with fractional impact. On the other hand, it's an extra shot at the most motivational word we have.

So here's another way to get extra mileage out of our favorite word. Suppose we have this sentence in our selling text:

> *That way you'll take advantage of the Preferred Buyer Group Discount.*

The word *you'll* is in there. Now, what else can we do with it to make it congruent with the Me-Myself-I Rule? This:

> *That way you'll take advantage of your Preferred Buyer Group Discount.*

The extra involvement device costs you nothing, so why not use it?

Hit The Target You're Aiming At

Check words for aim and redirect if they're off-target for the reader you're trying to reach.

As you start creating your message, write on a sheet of scratch paper: "This message is aimed at [GENERIC NAME OF GROUP]." Keep that note visible as you write and you decrease the possibility of firing across their bow instead of smack into their mizzenmasts.

A mailer from a leasing company to automobile dealers:

> *You can see how leasing increases the possibility of buying a more luxurious automobile.*

Wrong target. Dealers aren't interested in buying. They're interested in *selling*. Let's tell them so:

You can see how leasing increases the possibility of your selling a more luxurious automobile.

Keep asking: What does my quarry want? You may miss a few words, but every one you replace parallels stripping out a rhinestone and inserting a diamond.

The Difference Between *We* and *I*

We establishes a corporate position; *I* makes a commitment.

The interchangeable use of *we* and *I* can confound even the most polished communicator. Which should we use?

The individual-in-contact (for example, the letter writer or spokesperson) has *position*. That's why an "I'm Whoever" opens a verbal message and a signature ends a written message. So an "I" reference transmits a personal pledge to a relationship.

The organization has *stature*. That's why a "we" reference says to the reader, "Our corporate integrity is on the line."

I is more personal than *we*, and the two aren't interchangeable—a benefit for the communicator, who can shift back and forth at will.

The "We-to-You" Shift

As so many examples have illustrated, most force-communication messages can't get hurt by shifting emphasis to *you* from *they*.

How about *you* instead of *I* or *we*? Not so automatic. Think back to the most famous advertisement of all time:

"They Laughed When I Sat Down at the Piano."

What power *I* has as surrogate for *You*. How uncomfortable many readers would have been had the ad been worded, "Do They Laugh When You Sit Down at the Piano?"

The word *I* makes it impossible for the reader or listener to think you're preaching, so it defangs hostility. Let's sophisticate the concept.

"You may have thought [WHATEVER], but you're wrong" will alienate as many potential buyers as it attracts. "I used to think [WHATEVER], but I was wrong" replaces venom with empathy-gathering nectar. "She used to think [WHATEVER], but she was wrong" establishes a buyer-judgmental position.

An oblique byway: A *we* to *you* shift when suggesting decisions is a mildly impelling guilt generator.

This one isn't easy to explain, but it's easy to demonstrate. Suppose we have this sentence:

It'll take just 10 seconds for you to indicate on the card whether we should keep you on our mailing list.

The *we* to *you* shift generates a change:

Take 10 seconds to indicate on the card whether you want us to keep you on our mailing list.

This now becomes a simple decision. Will your target feel more guilt if he or she doesn't make the indication on the card, because "you want us to" moves the decision-making? Fraction-ally, you say? Then why not use it?

Consider alternatives before making an automatic "you" deci-sion. We have lots of choices besides *You: I, We, He, She, Them. You* demands involvement; *He, She,* or *Them* requests analysis. *I* or *We* asks for reader judgment. Which should you use?

The answer to that universal question isn't universal. What if the question had been, "Which should the communicator use?" Can you see at once how the shift takes *you* off the hotseat and puts you in an analytical posture?

You're usually safe with *you*. But *usually* proves: Knowing exceptions makes you a more effective communicator.

Changing Message Thrust by Subject Choice

The choice of subject is the key to emphasis as the reader or listener interprets the message thrust:

"Your project probably never will be finished" is less combat-ive than "You probably will never finish your project," because emphasis is on the project, not you. (Changing the first statement from passive to active—"Your project probably will never see its completion"—has no effect on comparative emphasis.)

Which Person? Victim or Perpetrator

This suggestion is primarily for fund-raisers, but applications occur in most forms of force-communication. If you've been emphasizing victims instead of perpetrators, consider the differ-ence between the two sides of a catastrophe, disaster, illness, or crime:

Victims are passive; perpetrators, whether human, mechanical, or forces of nature, are active. Since active is more emotional—and therefore more dynamic—and therefore more likely to cause the reader to take pen in hand or lift the phone much—of what you write can benefit from role-reversal. Which has greater impact?

So far this year, 656 helpless bicyclists have been killed by careless motorists.

or—

So far this year, careless motorists have killed 656 helpless bicyclists.

Right! The active voice of killing makes carelessness more dramatic. This also applies to storms, buildings, and cigarette smokers.

Involvement Means Responsibility

If you're a *you*-user, get some mileage out of the word. One way is to put action responsibility onto the message recipient's shoulders.

The power communicator never gives up on this dogma, even though so many salespeople have a clerk-like mentality; they think they can get action without suggesting action.

The shift is as simple as changing passive voice to active voice. For example, the industrial supply company whose mailer suggests—

For tools you want added to your kit

might find more dynamite in the effortless change to—

For tools you want to add to your kit

or the even more responsibility-invoking—

For tools you should have in your tool kit

because the second approach suggests pre-decided reader reaction and the third suggests reader *action*, not waiting for something to happen. Indolence and apathy are our enemies, and we not only shouldn't feed them; we should cut off their air.

The Giant Leap: From "Ours" to "Yours"

Whether selling or convincing, the challenge is getting other persons to accept "ours" as "theirs."

That's what the professional communicator does for a living.

Chapter 12
Potpourri

S ome types of power communication don't fit any specific category. They just exist, and this chapter is the launching-pad for the hundreds or even thousands you'll discover, use, and if you're statesmanlike, share.

This chapter is also a logical self-review, to keep your analytical powers razor-sharp.

No Magi Behind This Gift!

What's wrong with this opening sentence of a subscription letter?

You are among a very small group of women invited to use this Gift Certificate we've enclosed.

You don't see it? Don't worry about it. You'll still live a long and useful life.

But if you did catch two glitches, you'll live a long, useful, and *prosperous* life.

- Glitch 1: How can even a small group of women use the same certificate? Wording is too loose.
- Glitch 2: The word *use* isn't as positive or dynamic as half a dozen other words that come to mind without digging.

Time to be counted! Is your reaction, "You're nit-picking again?" If so, the concept of power communication hasn't yet taken firm root.

Is your reaction, "You didn't go far enough, because the word *group* denies exclusivity"? If so, consider yourself qualified to wear a Power Communicator T-shirt.

Where to Put the Phone Number

The Phone Number Positioning Rule:

- When you ask for "phone number" in the coupon or order form, put it after the space for "address," not before.

This is a subtle proposition because it deals in human motivation. Most people regard their addresses as public information, but many think their phone number should be private.

So if we hit them with a request for private information *before* we ask for public information, we might kill off the order. If you've been asking for the phone number early on, this is worth testing.

The Rule of Parallel Positioning

Word positioning is another minuscule indicator of professionalism. *The Rule of Parallel Positioning*:

- When a construction has parallel words, clarity calls for parallel positioning.

The would-be, the beginner, and the dilettante see nothing wrong with this copy:

Enjoy every bite first. Then . . .

The professional says, "Hold it. Paralleling the positions of the two parallel words, 'first' and 'then,' has to help this structure because it adds clarity." This writer changes the copy to read:

First, enjoy every bite. Then . . .

Communicating under the Rule of Parallel Positioning is as easy as thinking in terms of logical sequence—one, two, three, four.

Tying Time to NOW Adds Specificity

A tie to *now* gives time a specific start and end.

Seem abstruse? For that matter, does the phrase "Seem abstruse?" seem abstruse? In use, it becomes clear. Which has greater impact?

Next month . . .

or—

A month from now . . .

Imminence belongs to the "now" approach because the time relationship gets a free ride. Another example:

It's 3 o'clock. We leave at 4 o'clock.

or—

It's 3 o'clock. We leave an hour from now.

What impression are we trying to generate? Do we want to suggest we have ample time or not much time?

The "now" reference is a tie, pulling future closer to present. We don't always want to do this, but it's comforting to know we have a device to do it when we do want to. Changing the target individual's perception without changing the facts is what information optimizing is all about.

Results Outpull Problems

When projecting benefit, describing the result is stronger than describing the problem.

Problems are powerful lead-ins. But then what? We're selling solutions, not the problems themselves. Suppose we have as a provocative heading the single word "Buried?" Our reference is a person in a business office, buried under a pile of memos.

Once we've established the problem and begun our exposition of benefits, we're selling *results*. So this sentence—

> *You're no longer buried under that avalanche of written memos . . .*

has less dynamite in it than this sentence—

> *You're finally out from under that avalanche of written memos . . .*

The first sentence states elimination of the problem, and that's all; the second sentence states a positive result, the outcome of elimination of the problem.

The Commercial Terminology Enfeebler

Commercial terminology thins out the mystery and romance in an exclusivity-based sales argument.

Implicit in the very nature of exclusivity is the joy of being on the inside, of getting something nobody else can have.

So this wording—

Privately Recorded Inside Information on Cassettes . . .

is less effective than this wording—

Privately Recorded Inside Information . . .

because the word "Cassettes" adds a mundane, prosaic overtone.

Careful, now. Sure, we have to tell them they'll get cassettes. Otherwise they won't know whether or not they can play the things. But we don't tell them here. We don't, just as our lips are brushing, stop to gargle Listerine.

Keep romance and mystery at a high pitch and don't destroy the purity of flavor by adding Diet Chocolate to the Perrier of lyricism. Talk about shooting yourself in the foot! This will do it, and it's another example of what happens when the communicator's emotional blinders cut off peripheral vision, which might have made possible a view of what the reader wants to read.

If It's "Official" Keep the Tone Official

If you're mailing or announcing an "official" notice, don't let the tone get too warm.

OFFICIAL NOTICE

THIS IS YOUR OFFICIAL NOTIFICATION THAT YOU HAVE DEFINITELY BEEN AWARDED (TWO) OF THE ITEMS SHOWN BELOW AND YOU MUST CLAIM THEM IMMEDIATELY!

PRIZES • AWARDS	SENDER
$10,000.00 CASH	SWEEPSTAKES CLEARINGHOUSE
$ 1,000.00 CASH	1555 REGAL ROW
$200 SAVINGS CERTIFICATE	DALLAS, TX 75247
$100 U.S. SAVINGS BOND	ATTN: J. JOHNSTON

IMPORTANT

YOU **MUST** RESPOND BY PHONE OR RETURN THIS CARD BY 1/25 OR YOU WILL FORFEIT YOUR AWARDS.

PHONES WILL BE ANSWERED (24) HOURS A DAY (7) DAYS A WEEK

TO CLAIM YOUR PRIZE

1. FOR IMMEDIATE DELIVERY **CALL NOW**
(USING A TOUCH TONE PHONE - $2.50 per minute)
1-900-740-4442
OPERATORS WILL IDENTIFY YOUR PRIZES OR
2. FOR 8-WEEK DELIVERY RETURN THIS CARD WITH SELF-ADDRESSED STAMPED ENVELOPE TO SENDER.

ODDS OF WINNING ARE POSTED ON REVERSE AND NUMBER OF PRIZES DISTRIBUTED DURING THIS PROMOTION DEPEND UPON THE NUMBER OF ENTRIES. CASH PRIZES MAY BE SPENT WITHOUT RESTRICTION. U.S. SAVINGS BONDS WILL BE ISSUED IN WINNER'S NAME OR WINNER'S DESIGNEE. SAVINGS CERTIFICATES ARE GOOD EXCLUSIVELY TOWARDS MERCHANDISE PURCHASES FROM SENDER. FOR AN OFFICIAL LIST OF MAJOR PRIZE WINNERS NAMES WRITE TO SENDER SHOWN ABOVE.

Fig. 12.1

The word "official" has great power—if its ambience seems official. This postcard maintains the image throughout, by eliminating any conviviality. Note the wording: "You must (not You have to) respond (not answer) this card by 1/25 or you will forfeit (not lose) your awards." Every imperative is put in passive voice to avoid any overtone of a one-to-one relationship.

This is one of the keys to that magic word, *verisimilitude*. Stay in character. Always put yourself in the position of the message recipient: What if this actually *were* an official notice? How would it be worded?

It would be crisp. It would be direct. It would be thin on adjectives. It could only skirt conviviality, not lapse into it.

Speed formats (all those [SOMETHING]-Grams) depend on an official look for their impact. If you're considering testing these formats by retyping your standard "Dear Friend" letter onto the "Urgent Message" form, reconsider. Mismatch of copy and format damages credibility.

"So What?" Statements—Their Cause and Cure

Don't begin your communication with a "so what?" statement.

One of our most respected mailing list companies mailed an announcement of a list availability. The letter begins with an ugh: "Dear Sir/Madam:"—even though it's computer-addressed.

This is the first sentence of the letter:

Over **One Trillion Dollars** *is spent by manufacturing companies each year on materials, equipment and services.*

If you don't agree this is a classic "so what" opening, you either wrote this letter or don't depend on your wits for a living. Of what value is the undigested number?

Take a look at the letter you're about to mail . . . the ad you're about to insert . . . the commercial you're about to record . . . the news release you're about to send to media. If the opening doesn't excite, does it at least nudge? If you're quoting a fact, will your target think the fact is relevant?

Accidentally Generating Antagonism . . . and How to Prevent It

Re-read a potentially sensitive communication from the viewpoint of a recipient who's looking for trouble.

Suppose somebody sent *you* a letter with this opening:

I know as well as you do that . . .

The writer has an even chance of generating antagonism, because in a heated debate, "I know as well as you do . . ." pops out when the other guy thinks you regard him as an ignoramus. Following the completely logical theory that one antagonistic party quickly transforms the other party into an antagonist, why risk misinterpretation? Safety almost always lies in the non-abrasive version:

I know, as you do, that . . .

What's the exception? When you want to project impatience or anger, aimed squarely at the target reader.

The Dangerous Power of Assumptive Claims

Is this ethical? You mail an offer. On its envelope you print, in a rubber stamp effect:

This is the information you asked for.

(Parenthetically, it's "asked for," not the stand-offish "requested.")

The person to whom you send the mailing not only didn't ask for it; she never heard of you.

Is *this* ethical? You mail a catalog. On its face or wrapper is this legend:

We're sorry, but unless you order something—
anything—*this is the last catalog we can send you.*

This is the first time you've sent a catalog to this person. So the first catalog is also the last catalog?

One more: Is *this* ethical? Your telemarketing pitch begins:

We talked a few months ago and you told me to call back about now.

or—

Did you have an opportunity to look over the information we mailed you?

The person fumbling with his memory on the other end of the phone can't remember . . . because this is the first contact.

Ethical? We have three possible answers:

1. Ethics don't apply to a sales situation in which the "sellee" sustains no damage. Each of these representations is designed to generate a combination of guilt and uncertainty, venerable and still-effective sales tactics.
2. The first example—"This is the information you asked for" is borderline. The second example— "This is the last catalog we can send you" has no ethical problems. The third example—"You told me to call back" and "Did you have the opportunity to look over the information we sent you?"—are unethical because they're outright lies.
3. All misrepresentation is unethical.

As communicator/marketer, it's your call. A computer software company which switches its service-call line from an 800 number to a 900 number, then puts the call on "hold" while the caller pays by the minute, is to many observers (especially those who have fallen victim to this procedure) far more unethical than cunning sales techniques.

The seller makes a decision: The potential sellee will/won't be damaged by mild misrepresentation, affirmative puffery, or largely untrue competitive claims. The company itself will/won't care about Buyer Remorse Syndrome or loss of goodwill among those who never would have bought anyway.

Long-range marketing philosophy or short-range marketing philosophy? It's your call . . . remembering that nuclear fallout can affect the health of other, more careful civilizations.

Suggesting Enablement

Suggesting enablement adds value to what you're selling . . . but the concept has a qualifier. The technique is tied to *would*—a conditional beginning. Typical writing: "How would you like to charge your next tank of gas to Universal Oil?" "How would you like to spend a weekend at Jamaica's most posh resort?" "Wouldn't you enjoy speaking French in France?"

The same openings, with the turbo-effect of enablement: "How would you like to be able to charge your next tank of gas to Universal Oil?" "How would you like to be able to spend a weekend at Jamaica's most posh resort?" "Wouldn't you enjoy being able to speak French in France?"

The benefit: Whatever we're selling provides enablement.

The caution: If what we sell provides enablement, implicitly we suggest prior *lack* of enablement. Choose targets carefully, because implication of inability, improperly couched or improperly aimed, can infuriate your target reader.

What if you reword, eliminating the power-safeguard *How*: "Would you like to be able to charge your next tank of gas to Universal Oil?" "Would you like to be able to spend a weekend at Jamaica's most posh resort?" "Would you enjoy being able to speak French in France?"

Salesmanship disappears. The question is milder and weaker, lacking leadership, because replacing "How would" with "Would" drains out the sales psychology. We no longer have a sales argument; instead, we have an unimproved question to which our target easily can answer, "No."

"Doubling": Helping the Target to Agree

"Doubling" helps the reader or listener to agree by changing a challenge/statement to a concur/suggestion. Doubling in question form eliminates rejection. Doubling exists in two principal forms, the question *ending* and the question *beginning*: Instead of "You've never touched precious stones so smooth," it's "You've never touched precious stones so smooth, have you?" Or "Have you ever touched precious stones as smooth as these?" Instead of "You've heard what the experts say," it's "You've heard what the experts say, haven't you?" or "Have you heard what the experts say?" Or "Haven't you heard what the experts say?"

Words Suggesting Stature

Words such as *preferred, status, select, priority, best possible, reserved, elect, select, chosen,* and *elite* implicitly underscore the "Only you" approach. One facet of the power within these words is the potential threat of losing status. The writer aware of *exclusivity* as a motivator also is aware of a standard human trait: fear of status-loss.

WARNING: Don't overuse artificial conferring of status within the same message. Overuse becomes toadying, which damages both acceptance of the status-claim and credibility.

"Less Is More" Verisimilitude

Specificity and credibility are Siamese twins. Inbred, they produce verisimilitude. So less can be more. Three examples:

1. Which has greater specificity? Which has greater credibility? A lifetime warranty or a 20-Year warranty? A 20-year warranty may be stronger than a lifetime warranty. "20" is specific and credible; "lifetime" is nonspecific and less credible.
2. "He'll bring more than 20 years of experience to your office" seems experienced; "He'll bring more than 40 years of experience to your office" seems old.
3. A reader or listener is more likely to accept "I made $34,000 this month" than "I made $40,000 this month," because $40,000 is a rounded-off number, not as *apparently specific* as $34,000.

Finally Adds Distance to a Negative Relationship

Adding the word *Finally* before a concluding negative makes the negative more dire, because it keeps the relationship at arm's length. **Example:**

[Finally,] I'm reluctant to issue more credit, because your slow processing of bills presents a problem.

"Finally" adds distance to the communication, making reader assumption of an ongoing relationship less likely.

"Therefore" and "However": Search and Destroy

For the power copywriter, the rule for using the word *therefore* couldn't be easier: Don't use it.

Can you think of *any* communication in which the word *therefore* adds any power at all? It's an antiquated pomposity, reserved for politicians and pedants.

However doesn't deserve quite such a severe dismissal; it ranks with *indeed* as an arm's-length, running-in-place word.

The power communicator knows the versatility of *so* and *but* as replacements (both are discussed elsewhere in this text).

Controlling Recency

How recent is *recent*? It's no news that the writer can control the degree of recency by word choice. But of greater value to the power communicator is recognition of verbiage which suggests recency but can't be nailed to the cross of false claims.

Suppose you've written a sales message with wording such as, "Recently a dealer declared his entire inventory obsolete and replaced it with these."

You wrote that two years ago. You want to keep using it, but your sense of integrity says "recently" misstates the time frame. What alternatives do you have?

For the next two years, "Not long ago" is a sensible replacement. "Not long ago" leans on children's fiction ("Long ago and far away . . .") as its paralleling touchstone. So the apparent opposite of "Not long ago" is "Long ago," and the episode being described didn't happen long ago . . . so what else could it be but recent?

Two more years pass. Now what?

The next-in-line step into historicity: "A dealer once declared . . ."

Now the cream on this slice of power communication cake, the substitution you can use forever:

Perhaps [maybe] you remember that a dealer declared . . ."

Two parenthetical explanations:

1. "Maybe" is bracketed because an informal communication prefers this word to the more formal, ergo, more intellectualized—"perhaps."
2. The word "that" ("you remember that . . .") appears for congruency with the Clarity Commandment. Try the statement without it: The reader has to go over it twice to absorb the thought.

Match Up Your Rhetoric

A newsletter promotes itself:

We shall tip off our readers, every month . . .

The mismatch is "we shall" paired with "tip off." They aren't from the same universe. It's Liza Doolittle, half-finished.

Oh, yes, pure grammar calls for "We shall." Power communicators long ago abandoned the "We shall . . ." archaism, and with good reason: They're communicators, not fifth-grade English teachers.

Communicators. We're communicators. We set a tone and stick with it. That's a crucial component of the magic word *veri-*

similitude. So "tip off" is street-talk, completely acceptable in conversation *if* it doesn't look as though it were planted artificially.

The point: If we use "tip off" we have to use at least "We will" and preferably "We'll." Notice, please: It's we "have to," not we "must." Let's not break the mood with even one misused word.

While we're matching up words . . . be sure the verbs match the nouns. The more colorful the noun, the more careful you as writer have to be with the verb. Consistency of imagery gives nouns and verbs a synergistic effect: $1 + 1 = 3$.

An example is the noun *skyrocket*, a colorful noun which generates an immediate visual impact. In a business magazine, an advertiser used *skyrocket* to promote rotating displays. His wording:

> *This stand can be a skyrocket, pushing sales to extraordinary levels.*

Can you see how the verb *pushing* weakens the noun? Readers don't stop to analyze why; we do stop, and we see the miniflaw: skyrockets don't push. A primitive word change fixes it.

> *This stand can be a skyrocket, rocketing (or if the writer doesn't want a repeat, zooming or boosting) sales to extraordinary levels.*

Hooking ourselves to the fiery tail of the skyrocket instead of its blunted nose gives the whole sentence a lift. Images match, and word power is restored.

Adjectives to Add Luster and Reinforcement

An adjective can add luster. "Genuine leather" is more desirable than "leather." "A full quart" is a bigger quantity than "a quart" but less than "one full quart."

Add reinforcing adjectives to nouns which specify without selling. **Example:**

You Can Live to Be 100!
An Evening with Dr. Malcolm Will Show You How

Adding the *selling* adjective enhances the offer:

You Can Live to Be 100!
A Single Evening with Dr. Malcolm Will Show You How

Warning: Don't lard a message so thickly with adjectives that the recipient begins to doubt your sincerity.

Sooner or Later

It's Thursday. An event will happen 13 days from now. How do you position that event?

- "A week from next Wednesday" is soon.
- "Two weeks from yesterday" is considerably more distant.

The tie to forward or backward—ahead or behind—influences reaction to the words.

Showing Duration of Time

There is a difference between "Over the past seven years . . ." "During the past seven years . . ." and "Within the past seven years":

- "Over" suggests the beginning and end of a period of time.
- "During" suggests something happening which didn't happen before or after.
- "Within" suggests a slice of time from an ongoing activity.

So the financial institution which states, "Within the past seven years, Progress Bank has provided more than a billion dollars to homeowners," takes advantage of the slice-of-time suggestion. This is considerably stronger than, "Over the past seven years, Progress Bank has provided more than a billion dollars to homeowners" which suggests no operation before the past seven years.

For clarifying strength, and to suggest continuing success, add the word *alone*: "Within the past seven years alone, Progress Bank has provided more than a billion dollars to homeowners."

Since Suggests Time, Not Cause

Which of these is the most effective way of offering a free look? Which offers the least reader comfort? Which is most convincing?

Your first look is entirely at our risk, so why not take that look?

or—

Because your first look is entirely at our risk, why not take that look?

or—

Since your first look is entirely at our risk, why not take that look?

The second version offers the least reader comfort. Why? The first version is the most convincing. Why?

Yes, the third version is smoother reading than the first. No, the third version isn't preferable, because "since" suggests time, not cause. Using "since" to suggest cause is an artifice of language use. It's common but it does require reinterpretation of what follows.

Two suggestions:

1. Use *since* for time and *because* for cause.
2. "Because" *isn't* routinely positive, so check to determine whether dropping the word will make the message more affirmative.

Hit-and-Run Credibility

Too many writers violate *The Credibility Paradox* out of simple, everyday, ordinary laziness. The Paradox:

- Telling the reader "This is incredible" on a hit-and-run level may be the only credible statement in the sales argument.

Back up the statement "This is incredible" with an explanation (however thin) of why the incredible is actually credible.

The Call to Action: Tell the Reader What to Do

Challenging the target individual usually has greater power than an instructional approach, because a challenge more easily dovetails into this call to action: Tell the reader what to do.

So should we challenge or should we instruct? Which type of communication brings more action?

One of the delights of power communication is realizing it could be either. A challenge is likely to fail if the reader feels the challenge is difficult, expensive, or mis-aimed. Instruction is likely to fail if the reader feels she's being underestimated, overestimated, or patronized.

In any individual circumstance, deciding which approach probably will work best becomes an easier job when we tack on the second half: *Tell the reader what to do.*

When you have the time and the discipline, try writing a call to action both ways, including telling the reader what to do. Then read it over and decide: Is the "challenger" version too slam-bang? Is the "instructor" version too pedantic?

The recipient of your message isn't interested in *what it does;* interest is in *what it does for me.* Offhand, we'd expect this truism to be more congruent with *challenge* than with *instruction;* and in most selling situations it is. But how about copy for computer software?

Match your approach to your target, not to what's easiest to write.

How Aggressive Should You Be?

Aggressive rhetoric can generate antagonisms. Asking permission avoids antagonisms but suggests a position lower than the reader's.

Example—a publisher's "lift" letter (a common additional enclosure in subscription mailings). An aggressive opening:

I want to add a personal note.

An opening which asks permission:

May I add a personal note?

Neither is objectionable but neither can claim both dynamics and conviviality.

So what the power communicator write? One possibility is the "bubbling over with enthusiasm" opening which sidesteps antagonisms by justifying its aggressive approach before projecting any sales argument. Example of the "bubbling overwith enthusiasm" opening:

I couldn't wait. I had to add my own personal note.

Men whose copywriting assignment is "Write like a woman" often use the "bubbling over with enthusiasm" technique, not just for the opening but for the entire communication. This artifice can lapse into gushiness, tiring for the reader. Over the next generation, as gender-differentials built on feminine daintiness and masculine macho fade, using bubbles to synthesize femininity probably will disappear. (See "Macho or Dainty," chapter 7.)

The Congruence Principle

A suggestion for those whose messages on the carrier envelope or whose first outcry in broadcast messages parallel "Flash!", "Stop!", or "Important!"—or predict earth-shattering news, about to follow.

If the reader opens an envelope or hears the rest of your commercial and is surprised by the rest of your message, the surprise should be a bonus payoff for that reader/listener. If not, you're generating antagonism.

Strong envelope copy and commercial openings generate a mood of receptivity. What follows should carry the same mood forward, not stop it in its tracks.

Let's call this *The Congruence Principle*:

■ Don't allow the fact to be a non sequitur after the announcement.

We get a piece of mail whose envelope screams, "URGENT! OPEN AT ONCE! LIFE OR DEATH INFORMATION!" What's inside?

If what's inside *is* urgent life or death information, no problem. The components are congruent. But suppose the mailer used all these attention getters, ignoring what he himself stuck into the envelope. In my opinion the reaction is one of having been bamboozled. It's a letdown, *reducing* response instead of *enhancing* it, unless . . .

. . .Unless within the first five seconds the reader spots a big benefit—a free offer, or a stupendous discount, or an "insider" offer.

Recognize the mood carryover from the moment the first impression hits to the moment the message is recognized. The mood is fragile, and the writer can strengthen it just as easily as the same writer can smash it.

The Benefit of Active-Possessive Wording

Active possessive is more salesworthy wording than active without possessive.

The words *possess* and *acquire* are too arm's-length formal for most direct response messages. So take a look at your thesaurus for synonyms. Wait, I'll save you the trouble. Here are a few:

own	capture
take	enjoy
seize	control
get	have

What these words have in common is their implicit assumption of the *result* of the buying transaction rather than the transaction itself. Applying this concept, we change this line:

Sporting goods stores can't buy it for as little as you can.

to this line—

Sporting goods stores can't get it for as little as you can.

The difference between "buy" and "get" is obvious: "Get" is "buy"-*plus*-result.

CAUTION: Easy does it: Don't go searching through every scrap of copy, wildly replacing *buy* with *get*. But consider replacing a word implying acquisition with a word implying ownership, especially in second or third references to the sale.

While we're on this point, "Lifetime Guarantee" isn't as potent as "Guaranteed for Your Lifetime" because the latter copy adds possession to the mix.

Informal = Less Threatening

The diminutive is less formal . . . and less formal is less threatening. So to project a friendlier image, use the diminutive.

For example, if you sign a business letter "Michael J. Brown," you'd type "Michael J. Brown"—but sign it "Michael Brown" or "Mike Brown," or even more informal (less formal?), "Mickey Brown." William Smith becomes Bill Smith, Eugene is Gene, Elizabeth becomes Betty, Barbara becomes Barb or Bobbie, Victoria becomes Vicki.

Obviously informality doesn't extend to dropping your communicative pants in public. The degree of informality, if any, depends on your relationship—or *desired* relationship— with the recipient.

Personalize to Keep Open
The Lines of Communication

Personalization takes the venom out of a verbal wasp bite. I've never understood why so many communications practitioners demand personalization in solicitation mailings but feel uncomfortable personalizing other elements.

Even in adversary relationships, the one-on-one impression keeps the lines open; the corporate voice approach helps keep the lines closed.

Which of these openings will bring the most results?

This is your last notice.

or—

I've been authorized to send this one last notice to you.

The difference between the message couchings is the difference between generating a defensive attitude and hatching an always-latent feeling of guilt. Guilt is a response motivator; annoyance isn't.

An Unpleasant Use of *Please*

Using the word *please* as a follower instead of a leader transforms a request to a symbol of either anger or superiority.
Note the difference between these two constructions:

Please remove this table.

Remove this table, please.

Please-following can be helpful when establishing (however subliminally) the relationship with another person. "Please answer me" may or may not result in an answer. "Answer me, please" is a more imperious command.

The Restoration/Preservation Rule

Suppose you have a hair restorer. Your illustration shows a model or a celebrity or a user . . . who has a full head of hair. Your advertising copy reads:

John Jones had a full head of hair when he was 20 years old. At age 57, he still does.

It's not bad selling copy, but put yourself in the balding position of your best prospects, and you'll make this copy change:

John Jones had a full head of hair when he was 20 years old. At age 57, he has a full head of hair again.

The difference clarifies itself when you relate your sales argument to the reader's attitude. No matter how strong the rest of your copy might be, the first headline suggests that John Jones might have lucky genes; his follicles are undisturbed by time. The second approach ties itself positively to what you're selling, not to the forces of nature.

So we have *The Restoration/Preservation Rule*:

- When promoting personal improvement products, restoration outpulls preservation.

Celebrity endorsers don't like this, because they prefer to project an unbroken image line. But readers do like it. They respond because they've lost something, not because they *might* lose it. So don't let a celebrity's business agent rewrite your copy.

The Benefits of Answering Your Own Question

Asking a question and then answering it has two benefits:

1. Questions seem to put the writer in the reader's position. The reader is led to think this is a question he might have asked, which reduces skepticism.
2. The writer increases the image of honesty, and reader rapport becomes more likely. The most common way of injecting a question is adding "Why? Because . . ." *in front of* a validating statement. The informational core changes not a whit; the relationship between writer and reader is upgraded.

Opening a Question with a Positive Statement

Opening a question with a positive statement directs the answer:

This is yours, isn't it?

instead of—

Isn't this yours?

The statement dominates the question, telling the message recipient what the answer should be, so resistance seems defensive.

L'Envoi

Even if you disagree with some of the proposed power enhancers in this book, you wouldn't have picked your way through its rhetorical labyrinth unless you agree. . . .

We're finally shaping and hardening some mini-rules for what has been, until the early 1990s, seat-of-the-pants creative decision-making.

Does application of cold-blooded rules sap romance out of our poetic fingertips?

These mild rules don't stifle creativity; no, they stifle chaos. We're word-surgeons, and knowing where to cut and how to stitch can save the communicator's equivalent of human life: spilled promotional dollars.

Information optimizing is an art beyond simple word-after-word placement. Yes, the art of communication *is* transforming itself into a science, even as we watch and participate. But here, in the exalted field of information optimizing, the writer will forever have the opportunity to underscore personal superiority as a wordsmith.

Chapter 13
Compendium of Power Communication Rules

Many of the principles in this book have been codified as "rules." But recognize two truths:

1. No rule is absolute.
2. Rules change as society changes.

The rules outlined in this book are presented here (alphabetized by the first key word) in condensed form. Chapter references enable the reader to check rules for exceptions and elaborations.

- **The Automatic <u>Authentication</u> Technique** (chapter 4)
  Authenticate by adding the mantle of apparent importance.

- **The <u>Ballooning Number</u> Rule** (chapter 2)
  The farther a number rises beyond the average individual's personal experiential background, the less emotion the number generates.

- **The John F. Kennedy <u>Buyer Attitude</u> Truism Rule** (chapter 3)
  In this Age of Skepticism, the prospective buyer's first question isn't "What will it do?" but "What will it do for me?"

- **The Rule of <u>Capitalization</u>** (chapter 10)
  Capitalize for importance.

- **The Clarity Commandment** (chapter 1)
  In force-communication, clarity is paramount. Don't let any other component of the communications mix interfere with it.

- **The Law of Comparative Advertising** (chapter 8)
  If you're number 2 or smaller, attack a specific. If you're number 1, ridicule generic opposition; don't single out or respond to one target. Be certain your comparison caters to the reader's question: "What's in it for me?"

- **The Comparative Superiority of Superiors Rule** (chapter 8)
  When comparing yours with theirs, use words suggesting superiority rather than difference.

- **The Rule of Condition Injection-Rejection** (chapter 10)
  Conditions weaken a message.

- **The Congruence Principle** (chapter 12)
  Don't allow the fact to be a nonsequitur after the announcement.

- **The Connotation Rule** (chapter 6)
  Substitute words and phrases with a positive connotation for words and phrases with a neutral or negative connotation.

- **The Credibility Paradox** (chapter 12)
  Telling the reader "This is incredible" on a hit-and-run level may be the only credible statement in the sales argument.

- **The Dynamic Reaction Rule** (chapter 10)
  If you want to generate a dynamic reaction, use dynamic words. If you want to generate an observer reaction, use colorless words.

- **The Bulk Non-Exclusivity Rule** (chapter 5)
  Bulk excludes exclusivity.

- **The Formality Rule** (chapter 4)
  All formal statements fail as throwaways.

- **The "Free" Effectiveness Rule** (chapter 12)
  The lower down the economic scale we go, the more effective the word *free* becomes.

- **The Generic Determination Rule** (chapter 2)
  The generic determines reaction more than the number.

- **The Rule of Hyperbole Diminution** (chapter 8)
  The better your prospect matches what you have to sell, the farther you'll drive him off by useless hyperbole.

- **The Rule of Acceptable Imperative** (chapter 7)
  The degree of acceptable imperative depends on the message recipient's view of the relationship with the message sender.

- **The Rule of Increasing Imperative** (chapter 11)
  The degree of imperative can increase as the text of a communication to those who aren't captive readers or listeners progresses.

- **The Rule of "Importance" Projection** (chapter 11)
  A scream of importance loses impact in ratio to the dominance of "We" references over "You" references following the scream.

- **The Rule of Individual Pinpointing or Group Avoidance** (chapter 5)
  Use a group reference when you want to downplay responsibility or depersonalize; use individual references when you want to emphasize responsibility or personalize.

- **The Rule of Jargon Conviviality** (chapter 1)
  If you want to connect with your reader, on convivial terms, use local argot . . . unless verisimilitude demands otherwise.

- **The "Mother, May I?" Rule** (chapter 11)
  Don't play "Mother, May I?" with your target unless he or she is preconditioned to accept you as a superior.

- **The Me-Myself-I Rule** (chapter 11)
  Your quarries care about themselves, not you; so get to the benefits fast.

- **The Rule of Negative Bleed-Over Effect** (chapter 6)
  The negative opening bleeds over to the reader's reaction to the advertiser.

- **The Negative Gear-Strip Probability** (chapter 6)
  Because negative headlines *always* require a gear-shift, getting to the point can be tortuous. The reader can't determine what the advertiser wants him to do.

- **The Negative Question Reversal** (chapter 6)
  Opening a *question* with "Don't you" automatically sways the reader or listener toward your point of view . . . the reverse of opening a statement with "Don't."

- **The Absolute Rule of Negative References** (chapter 6)
  Use a negative reference to whatever you're selling only if such a reference will help either salesworthiness, credibility, or both.

- **The First Subrule of Negative References** (chapter 6)
  Don't use positive words when you're trying to generate negative feelings.

- **The Rule of <u>Negative</u> Transmission** (chapter 6)
  Unless you want the reader or viewer to think you're the originator or generator of the reason for negative information, don't put this information aggressively.

- **The First Subrule of Negative Transmission** (chapter 6)
  Don't tell the reader, "You have a problem," unless you reassure him a little later on, "but I have the solution to your problem."

- **The Second Subrule of <u>Negative</u> Transmission** (chapter 6)
  Don't open a selling argument with "Don't." Save this word, which can kill rapport, until you've introduced a "Do . . ." for the reader to cling to.

- **The <u>Negative</u> Validation Rule** (chapter 6)
  Negatives validate the positives.

- **The Rule of <u>Noun</u> Dominance** (chapter 9)
  Nouns overpower adjectives.

- **The Rule of <u>Numerical Manipulation</u>** (chapter 2)
  Deciding whether to break numbers into component fragments or pile them into totals depends on whether you want your target to think he/she is spending money or getting money.

- **The Subrule of <u>Numerical Manipulation</u>** (chapter 2)
  If the total number gives greater greed satisfaction than the immediacy of the daily number, go with the total number.

- **The Rule of <u>Overuse</u>** (chapter 2)
  Overuse = Abuse.

- **The Oxymoron Reaction Rule** (chapter 10)
  When your oxymoron causes a double-take you're a winner. When people laugh at your oxymoron—and you didn't intend to generate laughter—you're a loser.

- **The Rule of Parallel Positioning** (chapter 12)
  When a construction has parallel words, clarity calls for parallel positioning.

- **The Rule of Percentile Feebleness** (chapter 2)
  Unless the numerical amounts are tiny, actual numbers have greater impact than percentages.

- **The Phone Number Positioning Rule** (chapter 12)
  When you ask for "phone number" in the coupon or order form, put it after the space for "address," not before.

- **The Pinpoint Description Rule** (chapter 3)
  Within the sought target-group, specificity attracts; outside the target-group, specificity may repel.

- **The Positive Superiority Principle** (chapter 6)
  Positives usually outpull negatives. So don't start your selling argument with "Don't."

- **The Peripheral Pussyfooting Weakener Rule** (chapter 10)
  Writing around a point drains excitement out. A message loses impact in direct ratio to the percentage of information given indirectly instead of directly.

- **The Agreement-Seeking Question Rule** (chapter 12)
  Adding an agreement-seeking question to the end of a claim makes the reader your partner.

- **The Quotation Mark Rule** (chapter 2)
Putting quotation marks around a word or phrase the reader may not recognize tells the reader we share the novelty of the idea . . . and helps him or her accept the unknown. Without the quotation marks, we say to the reader, "We know something you don't."

- **The Rule of Key Word Repetition** (chapter 10)
If you have to re-use a word in speech or writing, emphasize the key word before its second use to show the reader the repeat is intentional.

- **The Restoration/Preservation Rule** (chapter 12)
When promoting personal improvement products, restoration outpulls preservation.

- **The Self-Serving Reader Rule** (chapter 7)
Assume the reader will interpret a word in its most common meaning, especially if the interpretation benefits the reader or lowers your image.

- **The Seller/Buyer Differential** (chapter 3)
The seller's concern: What it is. The buyer's concern: What it will do for him.

- **The Rule of Singulars** (chapter 5)
When claiming exclusivity, stay in sync by using singular instead of plural.

- **The Rule of Statistical Deficiency** (chapter 2)
Readers respond less to cold-blooded statistics than they do to warm-blooded examples.

- **The Superlative Identification Rule** (chapter 3)
The superlative can help identify.

- **The Argumentative Supremacy Truism** (chapter 11)
  "What's in it for me?" is paramount, over any other component of the sales argument. To the message-recipient, the
  rationale behind the offer is inconsequential.

- **The Sweepstakes Numbering Rule** (chapter 2)
  In sweepstakes copy, use as many zeros as you can.

- **The Law of Tenses** (chapter 5)
  Present tense outsells future tense because the present is now,
  and your reader wants benefits now.

- **The Exception to The Law of Tenses** (chapter 5)
  Tying future to present tells the reader: "This will be for all
  eternity."

- **The First Touchstone Rule** (chapter 8)
  To be effective, the touchstone should be recognized by the
  reader.

- **The Second Touchstone Rule** (chapter 8)
  If the touchstone is actually within the reader's experiential
  background, impact and credibility increase in direct ratio to
  emotional acceptance of the memory.

- **The Dynamic Unisex Rule** (chapter 7)
  The more dynamic the message, the smaller the differential
  between masculine and feminine writing.

- **The Rule of Indirect Weakness** (chapter 6)
  The less harsh and direct the message, the less powerful
  it is.

■ **The Rule of You, Me, and Us** (chapter 5)
The sales wallop of "You" as recognizable target is fractional compared to "You" as decision-maker. The vendor should hold back the implication that he takes the reader's reaction for granted until his sales argument reaches the point of "Watch it, you could miss out."

A Final Suggestion

Your computer or word processor has a wonderful key. It's the one you use to *search*.

Skipping through this book, most readers—certainly including the author—see words and constructions we shouldn't be using but find, too often, in our own messages.

Make a list of the ones you recognize. Your list might include "of the . . ." and "who is . . ." phrases or *needs* as a noun or a pet cliché or words drawing no image (*quality* and *service*, for example).

Whatever they are, tape the list to your keyboard. Then, for each of the next half-dozen messages, search for them before printing.

The results will be worth it, on two levels:

1. your message-transmission will be stronger;
2. the exercise will vaccinate you against these pests so you can go on to eradicate others.

Good luck to us all!

Index